The Fair Maid of the Inn by John Fletcher

The play was licensed by the Master of the Revels some 6 months after the death of Fletcher in August 1626. The play is thought to have been unfinished at the time of Fletcher's death and was completed and reworked by a variety of collaborators most likely to include (but perhaps not limited to) Philip Massinger, John Webster & John Ford.

John Fletcher was born in December, 1579 in Rye, Sussex. He was baptised on December 20th.

As can be imagined details of much of his life and career have not survived and, accordingly, only a very brief indication of his life and works can be given.

Young Fletcher appears at the very young age of eleven to have entered Corpus Christi College at Cambridge University in 1591. There are no records that he ever took a degree but there is some small evidence that he was being prepared for a career in the church.

However what is clear is that this was soon abandoned as he joined the stream of people who would leave University and decamp to the more bohemian life of commercial theatre in London.

The upbringing of the now teenage Fletcher and his seven siblings now passed to his paternal uncle, the poet and minor official Giles Fletcher. Giles, who had the patronage of the Earl of Essex may have been a liability rather than an advantage to the young Fletcher. With Essex involved in the failed rebellion against Elizabeth Giles was also tainted.

By 1606 John Fletcher appears to have equipped himself with the talents to become a playwright. Initially this appears to have been for the Children of the Queen's Revels, then performing at the Blackfriars Theatre.

Fletcher's early career was marked by one significant failure; The Faithful Shepherdess, his adaptation of Giovanni Battista Guarini's Il Pastor Fido, which was performed by the Blackfriars Children in 1608.

By 1609, however, he had found his stride. With his collaborator John Beaumont, he wrote Philaster, which became a hit for the King's Men and began a profitable association between Fletcher and that company. Philaster appears also to have begun a trend for tragicomedy.

By the middle of the 1610s, Fletcher's plays had achieved a popularity that rivalled Shakespeare's and cemented the pre-eminence of the King's Men in Jacobean London. After his frequent early collaborator John Beaumont's early death in 1616, Fletcher continued working, both singly and in collaboration, until his own death in 1625. By that time, he had produced, or had been credited with, close to fifty plays.

Index of Contents

DRAMATIS PERSONAE
MEN
Duke of Florence.
Cesario, a young Gentleman of a fiery nature, Son to Alberto,
Alberto, Father to Cesario, Admiral of Florence.
Baptista, a brave Sea-Commander, antient friend to Alberto, and Father to Mentivole and Bianca.
Mentivole, Son to Baptista, Lover of Clarissa.
Prospero, a noble friend to Baptista.
Two Magistrates of Florence.
Host, the supposed Father to Bianca.
Forobosco, a cheating Mountebank.
Clown, the Mountebanks man, and setter.
Three Gentlemen.
Secretary to the Duke.
Dancer   } Four fools and knaves,
Taylor   } who pretend to love
Muletier   } Bianca, the Fair
Pedant   } Maid of the Inn.
Sailors.
WOMEN
Mariana, Wife to Albertus, a virtuous Lady.
Clarissa, Mariana's Daughter, in love with Mentivole.
Juliana, Niece to the Duke of Genoa, Baptista's second wife.
Bianca, the Fair Maid of the Inn, beloved of Cesario, and Daughter to Baptista and Juliana.
Hostess, the supposed Mother of Bianca.

THE SCENE: Florence

Plays have their fates, not as in their true sence
They're understood, but as the influence
Of idle custom, madly works upon
The dross of many tongu'd opinion.
A worthy story, howsoever writ
For Language, modest Mirth, Conceit or Wit,
Meets oftentimes with the sweet commendation
Of hang't, 'tis scurvy, when for approbation
A Jigg shall be clapt at, and every rhime
Prais'd and applauded by a clamorous chime.
Let ignorance and laughter dwell together,
They are beneath the Muses pity. Hither
Come nobler Judgements, and to those the strain
Of our invention is not bent in vain,
The Fair Maid of the Inn to you commends
Her hopes and welcomes, and withal intends
In th' Entertains to which she doth invite ye,
All things to please, and some things to delight ye.

ACTUS PRIMUS

SCÆNA PRIMA

Enter **CESARIO** and **CLARISSA**.

CESARIO
Interpret not Clarissa, my true zeal
In giving you counsel, to transcend the bounds
That should confine a brother; 'tis your honor,
And peace of mind (which honor last will leave you)
I labor to preserve, and though you yet are
Pure and untainted, and resolve to be so:
Having a Fathers eye, and Mothers care
In all your ways to keep you fair, and upright.
In which respects my best advices must
Appear superfluous; yet since love, dear Sister
Will sometimes tender things unnecessary,
Misconstrue not my purpose.

CLARISSA
Sir, I dare not:
But still receive it as a large addition,
To the much that I already stand ingag'd for,

Yet pardon me, though I profess upon
A true examination of my self,
Even to my private thoughts I cannot find
(Having such strong supporters to uphold me)
On what slight ground the least doubt can be rais'd
To render me suspected, I can fall,
Or from my Fame or Virtue.

CESARIO
Far be it from me,
To nourish such a thought; and yet excuse me,
As you would do a Lapidary, whose whole fortunes
Depend upon the safety of one Jewel,
If he think no case precious enough
To keep it in full lustre, nor no locks,
Though lending strength to Iron doors sufficient
To guard it, and secure him; you to me are
A Gemm of more esteem, and priz'd higher
Than Usurers do their Muck, or great men Title.
And any flaw (which heaven avert) in you,
(Whose reputation like a Diamond
Cut newly from the rock, women with envie,
And men with covetous desires look up at)
By prying eies discovered in a moment
Would render what the braveries of Florence
For want of counterpoize, forbear to cheapen,
Of little or no value.

CLARISSA
I see brother
The mark you shoot at, and much thank your love;
But for my Virgin Jewel which is brought
In comparison with your Diamond, rest assur'd
It shall not fall in such a workmans hands
Whose ignorance or malice shall have power
To cast one cloud upon it, but still keep
Her native splendor.

CESARIO
'Tis well, I commend you;
And study your advancement with that care
As I would do a Sisters, whom I love
With more than common order.

CLARISSA
That from me,
I hope's return'd to you.

CESARIO

I do confess it,
Yet let me tell you, (but still with that love,
I wish to increase between us) that you are
Observ'd against the gravity long maintain'd
In Italy (where to see a maid unmasqu'd
Is held a blemish) to be over-frequent
In giving or receiving visits.

CLARISSA

How?

CESARIO

Whereas the custom is here to wooe by Picture,
And never see the substance: you are fair,
And beauty draws temptations on; You know it,
I would not live to see a willing grant
From you, to one unworthy of your birth,
Feature or fortune; yet there have been Ladies
Of rank, proportion, and of means beyond you,
That have prov'd this no miracle.

CLARISSA

One unworthy?
Why, pray you gentle brother, who are they
That I vouchsafe these bounties to? I hope
In your strict Criticisme of me, and my manners,
That you will not deny they are your equals.

CESARIO

Angry?

CLARISSA

I have reason, but in cold blood tell me,
Had we not one Father?

CESARIO

Yes, and Mother too.

CLARISSA

And he a Soldier.

CESARIO

True.

CLARISSA

If I then borrow
A little of the boldness of his temper,

Imparting it to such as may deserve it;
(However indulgent to your selves, you brothers
Allow no part of freedom to your Sisters)
I hope 'twill not pass for a crime in me,
To grant access and speech to noble suitors;
And you escape for innocent, that descend
To a thing so far beneath you. Are you touch'd?
Why did you think that you had Giges Ring,
Or the Herb that gives invisibility?
Or that Bianca's name had ne'er been mention'd;
The fair Maid of the grand Osteria, brother.

CESARIO
No more.

CLARISSA
A little, brother. Your night walks,
And offer'd presents; which coy she, contemn'd,
Your combats in disguises with your Rivals,
Brave Muletiers. Scullions perfum'd with grease,
And such as cry meat for Cats must be remembred;
And all this pother for a common trull,
A tempting sign, and curiously set forth,
To draw in riotous guests, a thing expos'd
To every Ruffians rude assault; and subject
For a poor salary, to a rich mans lust,
Though made up of diseases.

CESARIO
Will you end yet?

CLARISSA
And this a Mistriss for Albertus Son,
One that I should call Sister?

CESARIO
Part not with
Your modesty in this violent heat; the truth is,
(For you shall be my Confessor) I love her,
But virtuously; report that gives her out
Only for fair, and adds not she is chaste,
Detracts much from her: for indeed she is,
Though of a low condition; compos'd
Of all those graces, dames of highest birth,
Though rich in natures bounties, should be proud of;
But leave her, and to you my nearest care,
My dearest best Clarissa. Do not think
(For then you wrong me) I wish you should live

A barren Virgin life; I rather aim at
A noble Husband, that may make you mother
Of many children, one that when I know him
Worth your embraces, I may serve, and sue to:
And therefore scorn not to acquaint me with
That man, that happy man; you please to favour.

CLARISSA
I ever purpos'd it, for I will like
With your allowance:

CESARIO
As a pawn of this;
Receive this Ring, but e'r you part with it
On any terms, be certain of your choice;
And make it known to me.

[Enter **SERVANTS** with Lights, **ALBERTO**, **BAPTISTA**, **MARIANA**, **MENTIVOLE**.

CLARISSA
You have my hand for't.

CESARIO
Which were it not my Sisters, I should kiss:
With too much heat.

CLARISSA
My Father and his guests, Sir.

ALBERTO
Oh my old friend, my tri'd friend, my Baptista:
These days of rest and feasting, sute not with
Our tougher natures, those were golden ones,
Which were enjoy'd at Sea; that's our true Mother:
The Land's to us a step-dame; there we sought
Honor, and wealth through dangers: yet those dangers
Delighted more than their rewards, though great ones,
And worth the undertakers: here we study
The Kitchin Arts, to sharpen appetite,
Dull'd with abundance; and dispute with Heaven;
If that the least puff of the rough North-wind,
Blast our times burthen, rendring to our Palats
The charming juice less pleasing; whereas there
If we had Bisket, powder'd flesh, fresh water,
We thought them Persian delicates, and for Musick
If a strong gale but made the main yard crack,
We danc'd to the loud Minstrel.

BAPTISTA
And fear'd less,
(So far we were in love with noble action)
A tempest than a calm.

ALBERTO
'Tis true Baptista;
There, there, from mutual aids lent to each other,
And virtuous emulation to exceed
In manly daring, the true School of friendship,
We learnt those principles, which confirm'd us friends
Never to be forgot.

BAPTISTA
Never I hope.

ALBERTO
We were married there, for bells the roaring Canon,
Aloud proclaim'd it lawful, and a prize
Then newly ta'en, and equally divided,
Serv'd as a dowry to you, then stil'd my wife;
And did enable me to be a Husband,
Fit to encounter so much wealth, though got
With bloud and horror.

MARIANA
If so got, 'tis fit Sir
Now you possess it, that you should enjoy it
In peace, and quiet; I, your Son, and Daughter
That reap the harvest of your winters labour,
Though debtors for it yet have often trembled,
When, in way of discourse, you have related
How you came by it.

ALBERTO
Trembled? how the softness
Of your sex may excuse you, I'll not argue,
But to the world, howe'er I hold thee noble
I should proclaim this boy some cowards bastard,
And not the Image of Albertus youth:
If when some wish'd occasion calls him forth,
To a brave trial, one weak artery
Of his, should show a fever, though grim death
Put on a thousand dreadful shapes to fright him;
The Elements, the Sea, and all the Winds
We number on our compass, then conspiring
To make the Scæne more ghastly; I must have thee
Sirrah, I must, If once you grapple with

An enemies ship, to board her, though you see
The desperate Gunner ready to give fire,
And blow the deck up, or like Cæsar's Soldier
Thy hands like his cut off, hang by the teeth,
And die undaunted.

MARIANA
I even die to hear you:
My son, my lov'd Cesario run such hazards?
Bless'd Saints forbid it: you have done enough
Already for one family, that rude way;
I'll keep him safe at home, and train him up
A compleat Courtier: may I live to see him,
By sweet discourse, and gracious demeanor,
Winn, and bring home a fair Wife, and a rich;
'Tis all I rest ambitious of.

ALBERTO
A Wife!
As if there were a course to purchase one
Prevailing more than honourable action!
Or any Intercessors move so far,
To take a Mistriss of a noble spirit,
As the true fame of glorious victories,
Atchiev'd by sweat and bloud! Oh the brave dames
Of warlike Genoua! they had eyes to see
The inward man, and only from his worth,
Courage, and conquests: the blind Archer knew
To head his shafts, or light his quenched Torch,
They were proof against them else.
No Carpet Knight
That spent his youth in Groves, or pleasant Bowers;
Or stretching on a Couch his lazy limbs,
Sung to his Lute such soft and melting Notes,
As Ovid, nor Anacreon ever knew,
Could work on them, nor once bewitch'd their sense;
Though he came so perfum'd as he had robb'd
Sabæa, or Arabia, of their wealth;
And stor'd it in one sute:
I still remember,
And still remember it with joy, Baptista,
When from the rescue of the Genoua Fleet,
Almost surpriz'd by the Venetian Gallies,
Thou didst return, and wert receiv'd in triumph.
How lovely in thy honor'd wounds and scars
Thou didst appear! what worlds of amorous glances
The beauties of the City (where they stood,
Fix'd like so many of the fairest stars)

Shot from their windows at thee! how it fir'd
Their blouds to see the enemies captive streams
Born through the streets! nor could chaste Juliana
The Duke's fair Neece, though guarded with her greatness
Resist this gallant charge, but laying by
Desparity of fortune from the object,
Yielded her self thy prisoner.

BAPTISTA
Pray you chuse some other theme.

MARIANA
Can there be one more pleasing?

BAPTISTA
That triumph drew on me a greater torture,
And 'tis in the remembrance little less
Than ever Captive suffer'd.

MARIANA
How? to gain the favour of so great a Lady?

BAPTISTA
Yes, since it prov'd fatal, t'have been happy, Madam,
Adds to calamity, and the heavy loss
Of her I durst not hope for, once enjoy'd,
Turns what you think a blessing to a curse,
Which grief would have forgotten.

ALBERTO
I am sorry I touch'd upon it.

MARIANA
I burn rather, Sir,
With a desire to hear the story of
Your loves, and shall receive it as a favour,
Which you may grant.

BAPTISTA
You must not be deny'd,
Yet with all brevity I must report it;
'Tis true, fair Juliana (Genoua's pride)
Enamour'd of my actions, lik'd my person;
Nor could I but with joy meet her affection;
Since it was lawful, for my first wife dead;
We were closely married, and for some few months
Tasted the fruits of't; but malicious fate,
Envying our too much happiness, wrought upon

A faithless servant, privy to our plot,
And Cabinet-Counselor to Juliana,
Who either for hope, or reward, or fear,
Discover'd us to the incensed Duke:
Whose rage made her close prisoner, and pronounc'd
On me perpetual banishment: some three years
I wander'd on the Seas, since entertain'd
By the great Duke of Florence; but what fate
Attended her? or Prospero my friend,
That staid at Genoua, to expect the issue,
Is yet uncertain.

[Enter a **GENTLEMAN**.

ALBERTO
From the Duke:

BAPTISTA
He's welcome, to end my forc'd relation.

ALBERTO
Signior Baptista;
The Great Dukes Will commands your present eare.

GENTLEMAN
It points indeed at both of you.

BAPTISTA
I wait it.

ALBERTO
In Mariana, to your rest.

BAPTISTA
Nay leave us, we must be private.

MARIANA
Stay not long Cesario:

[Exeunt Manet **CESARIO, MENTIVOLE**.

MENTIVOLE
So these old men vanish'd, 'tis allow'd
That we may speak, and howsoe'r they take
Delight in the discourse of former dangers,
It cannot hinder us to treat a little
Of present pleasures.

CESARIO
Which if well injoy'd,
Will not alone continue, but increase
In us their friendship.

MENTIVOLE
How shall we spend the night?
To snore it out like drunken Dutchmen, would
Sort ill with us Italians. We are made
Of other metall, fiery, quick, and active;
Shall we take our fortune? and while our cold fathers
(In whom long since their youthful heats were dead,)
Talk much of Mars, serve under Venus Ensigns,
And seek a Mistriss.

CESARIO
That's a game dear friend,
That does admit no rival in chase of it.
And either to be undertook alone,
Or not to be attempted.

MENTIVOLE
I'll not press you;
What other sports to entertain the time with
The following morning?

CESARIO
Any that may become us.

MENTIVOLE
Is the Neapolitan horse the Viceroy sent you,
In a fit plight to run?

CESARIO
So my Groom tells me.
I can boast little of my horsemanship;
Yet upon his assurance, I dare wager
A thousand Crowns, 'gainst any horse in Florence,
For an eight mile course.

MENTIVOLE
I would not win of you,
In respect you are impatient of loss:
Else I durst match him with my Barbary
For twice the sum.

CESARIO
You do well to excuse it, being certain to be beaten.

MENTIVOLE
Tush. You know the contrary.

CESARIO
To end the controversie
Put it to trial, by my life I'll meet you

[Enter **CLARISSA**.

With the next rising Sun.

MENTIVOLE
A match. But here
Appears a Cynthia, that scorns to borrow
A beam of light from the great eye of Heaven,
She being her self all brightness; how I envy
Those amorous smiles, those kisses, but sure chaste ones
Which she vouchsafes her brother!

CLARISSA
You are wanton:
Pray you think me not Bianca, leave I pray you;
My Mother will not sleep before she see you,
And since you know her tenderness, nay fondness;
In every circumstance that concerns your safety,
You are not equal to her.

CESARIO
I must leave you; but will not fail to meet you.

MENTIVOLE
Soft sleeps to you.

MARIANA [within}
Cesario.

CLARISSA
You are call'd again.

CESARIO
Some Sons
Complain of too much rigor in their Mothers;
I of too much indulgence; you will follow.—

[Exit.

CLARISSA

You are her first care, therefore lead the way.

MENTIVOLE
She staies: blest opportunity, she staies:
As she invited conference, she was ever
Noble, and free: but thus to tempt my frailty,
Argues a yielding in her; or contempt
Of all that I dare offer; stand I now
Consulting? No, I'll put it home.

CLARISSA
Who waits there? more Lights.

MENTIVOLE
You need them not, they are as useless,
As at noon-day; can there be darkness, where
Nature then wisely liberal, vouchsaf'd
To lend two Suns.

CLARISSA
Hyperboles:

MENTIVOLE
No, truths:
Truths beauteous Virgin, so my love-sick heart
Assures me, and my understanding tells me
I must approach them wisely, should I rashly
Press near their scorching beams, they would consume me
And on the contrary, should your disdain
Keep me at too much distance, and I want
Their comfortable heat, the frost of death
Would seize on all my faculties.

CLARISSA
Pray you pause, Sir.
This vehemency of discourse must else needs tire you.
These gay words take not me, 'tis simple faith
Honest integrity, and lawful flames
I am delighted with:

MENTIVOLE
Such I bring with me, and therefore Lady.

CLARISSA
But that you took me off
E're I came to a period; I had added
A long experience must be requir'd
Both of his faith and trust, with whom a Virgin

Trafficks for, what's dearest in this life,
Her liberty, and honor; I confess
I oft have view'd you with an eye of favour,
And with your generous parts the many tenders
Of doing me all fair offices, have won
A good opinion from me.

MENTIVOLE
Oh speak ever, I never heard such Musick.

CLARISSA
A plain tune, Sir:
But 'tis a hearty one; when I perceive
By evident proofs, your aims are truly noble,
And that you bring the Engines of fair Love,
Not of foul Lust, to shake and undermine
My Maiden-fortress: I may then make good
What now I dare not promise.

MENTIVOLE
You already
In taking notice of my poor deservings,
Have been magnificent, and 'twill appear
A frontless impudence to ask beyond this
Yet qualifie, though not excuse my error,
Though now I am ambitious to desire
A confirmation of it.

CLARISSA
So it wrong not my modesty to grant it.

MENTIVOLE
'Tis far from me,
I only am a suitor, you would grace me
With some toy, but made rich in that you wore it,
To warrant to the world that I usurp not
When I presume to stile my self your servant,
A ribond from your shooe:

CLARISSA
You are too humble,
I'll think upon't; and something of more value
Shall witness how I prize you, it grows late,
I'll bring you to the door.

MENTIVOLE
You still more bind me.—

[Exeunt.

[Enter **DUKE of FLORENCE, ALBERTO, BAPTISTA, MAGISTRATES,** and **ATTENDANTS.**

DUKE of FLORENCE
You find by this assur'd intelligence
The preparation of the Turke against us.
We have met him oft and beat him; now to fear him
Would argue want of courage, and I hold it
A safer policie for us and our signiories
To charge him in his passage o'er the Sea,
Than to expect him here.

ALBERTO
May it please your Highness
Since you vouchsafe to think me worthy of
This great imployment, if I may deliver
My judgement freely, 'tis not flattery
Though I say my opinion waits on you,
Nor would I give my suffrage and consent
To what you have propos'd, but that I know it
Worth the great speaker, though that the denial
Call'd on your heavy anger. For my self
I do profess thus much, if a blunt Soldier,
May borrow so much from the oyl'd tongu'd Courtier,
(That ecchoes whatsoe'er the Prince allows of)
All that my long experience hath taught me
That have spent three parts of my life at Sea,
(Let it not taste of arrogance that I say it)
Could not have added reasons of more weight
To fortifie your affections, than such
As your grace out of observation meerly
Already have propounded.

BAPTISTA
With the honor to give the daring enemy an affront
In being the first opposer it will teach
Your Soldiers boldness: and strike fear in them
That durst attempt you.

1ST MAGISTRATE
Victuals and Ammunition,
And Money too, the sinews of the War, are stor'd up in the
Magazine.

2ND MAGISTRATE
And the Gallies new rig'd and train'd up,
And at two dayes warning fit for the service.

DUKE of FLORENCE
We commend your care,
Nor will we e'er be wanting in Our counsels,
As we doubt not your action; you Baptista
Shall stay with us; that Merchant is not wise,
That ventures his whole fortunes in one bottom.
Albert. Be our Admiral, spare your thanks,
'Tis Merit in you that invites this honor,
Preserve it such; ere long you shall hear more,
Things rashly undertaken end as ill,
But great acts thrive when reason guides the will.

[Exeunt.

[Enter **THREE GENTLEMEN**.

1ST GENTLEMAN
No question 'twas not well done in Cæsario,
To cross the horse of young Mentivole
In the midst of this course.

2ND GENTLEMAN
That was not all, the switching him dull'd him.

3RD GENTLEMAN
Would that both the jades
Had broke their necks, when they first started; 'Slight,
We stand here prating, give them leave to whisper,
And when they have cut one anothers throats

[Enter **MENTIVOLE**, and **CESARIO**.

Make in to part 'em.

2ND GENTLEMAN
There is no such hazard,
Their Fathers friendship, and their love forbid it;
See where they come!

1ST GENTLEMAN
With fury in their looks.

MENTIVOLE
You have the wager, with what foul play got
I'll not dispute:

CESARIO

Foul play?

MENTIVOLE
I cannot speak it
In a fairer language, and if some respects
Familiar to my self chain'd not my tongue,
I should say no more. I should, but I'll sit down,
With this disgrace; how e'er press me no farther.
For if once more provok'd, you'll understand
I dare no more suffer an Injury,
Than I dare do one.

CESARIO
Why Sir are you injur'd
In that I take my right which I would force,
Should you detain it?

MENTIVOLE
Put it to judgment.

CESARIO
No; my will in this shall carry it.

MENTIVOLE
Your will? nay, farewell softness then.

[They suddenly draw

3ᴿᴰ GENTLEMAN
This I foresaw.

2ᴺᴰ GENTLEMAN
Hold, hold.

CESARIO
I am hurt.

2ᴺᴰ GENTLEMAN
Shift for your self, 'tis death.

1ˢᵀ GENTLEMAN
As you respect me, bear him off with care,
If he miscarry since he did the wrong,
I'll stand the shock of't.

2ᴺᴰ GENTLEMAN
Gently, he will faint else.—

[Exeunt **GENTLEMAN** with **CESARIO**.

MENTIVOLE
And speedily, I beseech you; my rage over,
That pour'd upon my reason clouds of error,
I see my folly, and at what dear loss
I have exchang'd a real innocence,
To gain a meer fantastical report,
Transported only by vain popular wind,
To be a daring, nay, fool-hardy Man.

[Enter **BAPTISTA**.

But could I satisfie my self within here,
How should I bear my fathers frown? They meet me,
My guilt conjures him hither.

BAPTISTA
Sirrah:

MENTIVOLE
Sir.

BAPTISTA
I have met the trophies of your ruffian sword:
Was there no other Anvile to make triall
How far thou durst be wicked, but the bosome
Of him, which under the adulterate name
Of friendship, thou hast murder'd.

MENTIVOLE
Murder'd Sir?
My dreams abhor so base a fact; true valour
Imploy'd to keep my reputation fair
From the austerest Judge, can never merit
To be branded with that title; you begot me
A man, no coward; and but call your youth
To memory, when injur'd, you could never
Boast of the Asses fortitude, slave-like patience:
And you might justly doubt I were your son,
If I should entertain it; if Cæsario
Recover, as I hope his wound's not mortal,
A second tryal of what I dare doe
In a just cause, shall give strong witness for me
I am the true heir to Baptista's courage,
As to his other fortunes.

BAPTISTA

Boy, to neither:
But on this strict condition, which intreaties
From Saints, nay Angels, shall not make me alter.
A friendship so began, and so continu'd
Between me and Alberto my best friend,
Your brawls shall not dissolve; it is my will,
And as I am thy Father, I command thee,
That instantly, on any termes, how poor
So e'er, it skills not, thou desire his pardon,
And bring assurance to me, he has sign'd it,
Or by my Fathers soul I'll never know thee:
But as a stranger to my blood; perform it,
And suddenly, without reply, I have said it.

MENTIVOLE
And in it given a heavier sentence on me
Than the most cruel death; you are my father
And your will to be serv'd, and not disputed
By me, that am your Son: But I'll obey,
And though my heart-strings crack for't, make it known,
When you command, my faculties are your own.

[Exeunt.

ACTUS SECUNDUS

SCÆNA PRIMA

Enter **ALBERTO**, **PHYSICIAN**, and a **SURGEON**.

PHYSICIAN
Have patience, Noble Sir; your son Cæsario
Will recover without question.

SURGEON
A slight wound.
Though it pierc't his body, it hath miss'd the vitals.

PHYSICIAN
My life for't, he shall take the air again within
these ten dayes.

ALBERTO
O but from a friend,
To receive this bloody measure from a friend!
If that a man should meet a violent death,

In a place where he had taken sanctuary,
Would it not grieve him? such all Florence held
Their friendship, and 'tis that which multiplies
The injury.

PHYSICIAN
Have patience worthy Signior.

ALBERTO
I do protest, as I am Man and Soldier,
If I had buried him in a wave at Sea,
(Lost in some honorable action)
I would not, to the saltness of his grave,
Have added the least tear; but these quarrels

[Enter **MARIANA**, and **CLARISSA**.

Bred out of game and wine, I had as live
He should have died of a Surfet.

MARIANA
Oh what comfort! How is it with our Son Sir?

ALBERTO
His Work-masters
Bear me in hand here, as my Lawyer does,
When I have a crackt Title, or bad Sute in Law,
All shall go well.

MARIANA
I pray you Gentlemen, what think you of his wound.

PHYSICIAN
'Tis but a scratch, nothing to danger.

CLARISSA
But he receiv'd it from a friend,
And the unkindness ta'en at that, may kill him.

MARIANA
Let me see him:

PHYSICIAN
By no means, he slumbers.

MARIANA
Then I cannot believe you,
When you tell me there's hope of him.

ALBERTO
Yet many Ladies
Do give more faith to their Physitian
Than to their Confessor.

CLARISSA
O my poor lost brother,
And friend more dear than Brother.

ALBERTO
More loud instruments
To disturb his slumbers! goe, goe, take Caroch:
And as you love me, you and the Girle retire
To our Summer house, i'th' Country; I'll be with you
Within these two days.

MARIANA
I am yours in all things,
Though with much sorrow to leave him.

[Exeunt **MARIANA, CLARISSA.**

ALBERTO
I pray you Gentlemen,
With best observance tend your Patient;
The loss of my heir-male, lies now a bleeding.

[Enter **MENTIVOLE.**

And think what payment his recovery
Shall show'r upon you,
Of all men breathing;

[Exeunt **PHYSICIAN, SURGEON.**

Wherefore do you arrive here? Are you mad?
My injury begins to bleed afresh
At sight of you; why this affront of yours
I receive more malitious than the other.
Your hurt was only danger to my son:
But your sight to me is death; Why come you hither?
Do you come to view the wounds, which you have made?
And glory in them?

MENTIVOLE
Rather worthy Sir, to pour Oyl into them.

ALBERTO

I am a Soldier Sir,
Least part of a Courtier, and understand
By your smooth Oyl,
Your present flattery.

MENTIVOLE

Sir, for my Fathers sake acknowledge me
To be born a Gentleman, no slave; I ever
Held flatterers of that breed; do not misconstrue
In your distaste of me, the true intent
Of my coming hither, for I do protest
I do not come to tell you I am sorry
For your sons hurt.

ALBERTO

Not sorry?

MENTIVOLE

No not sorry; I have to the lowest ebbe, lost all my fury:
But I must not lose my honesty; 'twas he
Gave heat unto the injury, which return'd
(Like a Petar, ill lighted, into 'th' bosome
Of him, gave fire to't) yet I hope his hurt,
Is not so dangerous, but he may recover;
When if it please him, call me to account,
For the loss of so much blood, I shall be ready
To do him noble reason.

ALBERTO

You are arm'd me thinks with wondrous confidence.

MENTIVOLE

O with the best Sir;
For I bring penitence, and satisfaction.

ALBERTO

Satisfaction? Why I heard you say but now,
You were not sorry for his wounds.

MENTIVOLE

Nor am I: the satisfaction which I bring Sir, is to you;
You are a Gentleman ne'er injur'd me;
One ever lov'd my Father, the right way,
And most approv'd of noble amity.
Yet I have run my sword quite through your heart,
And slightly hurt your son; for't may be fear'd,
A grief ta'en at these years for your sons loss,

May hazard yours: And therefore I am sent
By him that has most interest in your sorrow;
Who having chid me almost to the ruin
Of a disheritance, for violating
So continued and so sacred a friendship
Of 50 Winters standing: such a friendship,
That ever did continue like the spring;
Ne'er saw the fall o'th' leaf; by him I am sent
To say the wrong I have done Sir, is to you:
And that I have quite lost him for a Father,
Until I find your pardon; nay there follows
A weightier deprivation; his Estate
I could with a less number of sighs part with.
Fortune might attend my youth, and my deservings
In any Climate: but a Fathers blessing,
To settle and confirm that fortune, no where;
But only here. Your pardon, give me that;
And when you have done, kill me; for 'tis that
Takes from me the effect of excommunication;
A Fathers heavy curse.

ALBERTO
Nay, may that curse
Light on himself, for sending thee in this minute:
When I am grown as deaf to all compassion,
As the cruellest Sea-fight, or most horrid tempest.
That I had drown'd i'th' Sea a thousand duckets,
Thou hadst not made this visit: rash young man,
Thou tak'st me in an ill Planet, and hast cause
To curse thy Father; for I do protest,
If I had met thee in any part o'th' World,
But under my own roofe, I would have kill'd thee.

[Within there.—Enter **PHYSICIAN**, **SURGEON**, and **SERVANTS**.

Look you!
Here's a triumph sent for the death of your young Master.

SERVANT
Shall we kill him?

ALBERTO
No, I'll not be so unhospitable; but Sir,
By my life, I vow to take assurance from you,
That right hand never more shall strike my son.

MENTIVOLE
That will be easily protested.

ALBERTO
Not easily, when it must be exacted, and a bloody seal to't.
Bind him, and cut off's right hand presently:
Fair words shall never satisfie foul deeds.
Chop's hand off.

MENTIVOLE
You cannot be so unrighteous, to your own honor.

PHYSICIAN
O Sir, collect your self;
And recall your bloody purpose.

ALBERTO
My intents of this nature, do ever come to action.

SURGEON
Then I must fetch another stickler.—

[Exit.

ALBERTO
Yet I do grieve at heart;
And I do curse thy Father heartily,
That's the cause of my dishonor; sending thee
In such an hour, when I am apt for mischief:
Apt, as a Dutchman after a Sea-fight,
When his enemy kneels afore him; come dispatch.

PHYSICIAN
Intreat him, Noble Sir.

MENTIVOLE
You shall excuse me;
Whatsoever he dares do, that I dare suffer.

[Enter **CESARIO**, and **SURGEON**.

CESARIO
Oh Sir, for honors sake stay your foul purpose,
For if you do proceed thus cruelly,
There is no question in the wound you give him,
I shall bleed to death for't.

ALBERTO
Thou art not of my temper,
What I purpose, cannot be alter'd.

SERVANT
Sir; the Duke
With all speed expects you. You must instantly
Ship all your followers, and to sea.

ALBERTO
My blessing stay with thee upon this condition,
Take away his use of fighting; as thou hop'st
To be accounted for my son, perform't.—

[Exit.

CESARIO
You hear what I am injoyn'd to.

MENTIVOLE
Pray thee take it,
Only this ring, this best esteem'd Jewel:
I will not give't to'th' hangman chops it off;
It is too dear a relique. I'll remove it nearer my heart.

CESARIO
Ha, that Ring's my Sisters.
The Ring I injoyn'd her never part withal
Without my knowledge; come, Sir, we are friends
Pardon my fathers heat, and melancholy;
Two violent Fevers which he caught at Sea,
And cannot yet shake off: only one promise
I must injoyn you to, and seriously.
Hereafter you shall never draw a Sword
To the prejudice of my life.

MENTIVOLE
By my best hopes I shall not.

CESARIO
I pray deliver me your sword
On that condition.

MENTIVOLE
I shall Sir, may it hereafter
Ever fight on your part.

CESARIO
Noble Sir, I thank you;
But for performance of your vow, I intreat
Some gage from you.

MENTIVOLE
Any Sir.

CESARIO
Deliver me that ring.

MENTIVOLE
Ha, this Ring? indeed this Jewel binds me,
If you knew the vertue of it, never more
To draw my sword against you.

CESARIO
Therefore I will have it.

MENTIVOLE
You may not.

CESARIO
Come: you must.
I that by violence could take your hand,
Can inforce this from you; this is a token Sir,
That we may prove friends hereafter.
Fare you well.

PHYSICIAN
Why did you ceise his Sword Sir?

CESARIO
To perform what my Father bade me,
I have for the present ta'en away his
Use of fighting.

PHYSICIAN
Better so,
Than take that which your Father meant.

[Exeunt. Manet, **MENTIVOLE**.

MENTIVOLE
Was ever the like usage? O that Ring!
Dearer than life, Whither is honor fled?

CESARIO
Thou art unmanly in each part,
To seize my sword first, and then split my heart.

[Exit.

[Enter **HOST** and **CLOWN**.

HOST
Thy Master that lodges here in my Osteria,
Is a rare man of art, they say he's a Witch.

CLOWN
A Witch? Nay, he's one step of the Ladder to preferment higher, he is a Conjurer.

HOST
Is that his higher title?

CLOWN
Yes, I assure you, for a Conjurer is the Devils Master, and commands him; whereas a Witch is the Devils Prentice, and obeys him.

HOST
Bound Prentice to the Devil!

CLOWN
Bound and inroll'd I assure you, he cannot start; and therefore I would never wish any Gentleman to turn Witch.

HOST
Why Man?

CLOWN
Oh he loses his Gentility by it, the Devil in this case cannot help him, he must go to the Herald for new Armes believe it.

HOST
As I am true Inkeeper, yet a Gentleman born,
I'll ne'er turn Witch for that trick;
And thou hast been a great Traveller?

CLOWN
No indeed, not I Sir.

HOST
Come, you are modest.

CLOWN
No, I am not modest, for I told you a lye, that you might the better understand I have been a Traveller.

HOST
So Sir, they say your Master is a great Physitian too.

CLOWN

He was no fool told you that, I assure you.

HOST

And you have been in England? but they say,
Ladies in England take a great deal of Physick.

CLOWN

Both wayes on my reputation.

HOST

So 'tis to be understood:
But they say, Ladies there take Physick for fashion.

CLOWN

Yes Sir, and many times dye to keep fashion.

HOST

How? dye to keep fashion!

CLOWN

Yes, I have known a Lady sick of the small Pocks, onely to keep her face from Pitholes, take cold, strike
them in again, kick up the heels, and vanish.

HOST

There was kicking up the heels with a witness.

CLOWN

No Sir; I confess a good face has many times been the motive to the kicking up of the heels with a
witness: but this was not.

[Enter **HOSTESS**, and **BIANCA**.

HOST

Here comes my wife and daughter.

CLOWN

You have a prety commodity of this night-worm?

HOST

Why Man?

CLOWN

She is a pretty lure to draw custom to your ordinary.

HOST

Do'st think I keep her to that purpose?

CLOWN
When a Dove-house is empty, there is cuminseed used to purloine from the rest of the neighbors; in England you have several Adamants, to draw in spurs and rapiers; one keeps silk-worms in a Gallery: A Milliner has choice of Monkies, and Paraketoes; another shewes bawdy East-Indian Pictures, worse than ever were Aretines: a Goldsmith keeps his Wife wedged into his shop like a Mermaid, nothing of her to be seen (that's Woman) but her upper part.

HOST
Nothing but her upper part?

CLOWN
Nothing but her upper bodies, and he lives at the more hearts ease.

HOST
What's the reason?

CLOWN
Because her nether part can give no temptation; by your leave, Sir, I'll tend my Master, and instantly be with you for a cup of Cherally this hot weather.

HOST
A nimble pated Rascal, come hither Daughter,
When was Cesario here?

BIANCA
Sir, not this fortnight.

HOST
I do not like his visits, commonly
He comes by Owl-light, both the time and manner
Is suspitious; I do not like it.

BIANCA
Sir, the Gentleman
Is every way so noble, that you need not
Question his intent of coming, though you did;
Pray Sir preserve that good opinion of me,
That though the custome of the place I was born in,
Makes me familiar to every guest,
I shall in all things keep my self a stranger
To the vices they bring with them.

HOSTESS
Right my daughter:
She has the right strain of her Mother.

HOST
Of her Mother?

And I would speak, I know from whence she took it;
When I was as young, I was as honest.

HOSTESS
Leave your prating.
And study to be drunk; and abuse your guests over and over.

[Enter **FOROBOSCO** and **CLOWN**.

HOST
Peace Wife. My honorable guest.

FOROBOSCO
My indear'd Landlord?
And the rest o'th' complements o'th' house.

HOST
Breakfast is ready Sir;
It waites only the tide of your stomach.

CLOWN
And mine gapes for't like a stale Oyster.
Ere you go to bed, fail not of that I pray.

[Exeunt all but **FOROBOSCO** and **CLOWN**.

FOROBOSCO
We will instantly be with you;
Now we are all fellows.
Nine a Clock, and no Clyents come
Yet, sure thou do'st not set up bills enough.

CLOWN
I have set up bills in abundance.

FOROBOSCO
What Bills?

CLOWN
Marry for curing of all diseases,
Recovery of stoln goods,
And a thousand such impossibilities.

FOROBOSCO
The place is unlucky.

CLOWN

No certain, 'tis scarcity of mony; do not you hear the Lawyers complain of it? Men have as much Malice as ever they had to wrangle, but they have no Mony: Whither should this Mony be travell'd?

FOROBOSCO
To the Devil I think.

CLOWN
'Tis with his Cofferer I am certain, that's the Usurer.

FOROBOSCO
Our cheating does not prosper so well as it was wont to do.

CLOWN
No sure, why in England we coo'd cozen 'em as familiarly, as if we had travell'd with a Brief, or a Lottery.

FOROBOSCO
I'th' Low-countries we did pretty well.

CLOWN
So so: as long as we kept the Mop-headed butter-boxes sober; marry when they were drunk, then they grew buzards: You should have them reel their heads together, and deliberate; your Dutchman indeed, when he is foxt, is like a Fox; for when he's sunk in drink, quite earth to a Mans thinking, 'tis full Exchange time with him, then he's subtlest; but your Switzer, 'twas nothing to cheat him.

FOROBOSCO
Nothing?

CLOWN
No, nor conscience to be made of it; for since nature afore-hand cozen'd him of his wit, 'twas the less sin for us to cozen him of his Mony.

FOROBOSCO
But these Italians are more nimble-pated, we must have some new trick for them; I protest but that our Hostess's daughter is a sweet Lass, and draws great resort to'th' house, we were as good draw teeth a horseback.

CLOWN
I told 'em in the Market-place you could conjure, and no body would believe me: but ere long I will make 'em believe you can conjure with such a figuary.

FOROBOSCO
What language shall's conjure in? high Dutch I think, that's full i'th' mouth.

CLOWN
No, no, Spanish, that roars best; and will appear more dreadful.

FOROBOSCO
Prethee tell me thy conceit thou hast to gull them.

CLOWN
No, no, I will not stael it; but my dear Jews-trump, for thou art but my instrument, I am the plotter, and when we have cozen'd 'em most titely, thou shalt steal away the Inn-keepers daughter, I'll provide my self of another moveable: and we will most purely retire our selves to Geneva.

FOROBOSCO
Thou art the compass I sail by.

[Enter **BAPTISTA** and **MENTIVOLE**.

BAPTISTA
Was ever expectation of so Noble
A requital answered with such contumely!
A wild Numidian that had suck'd a Tigress,
Would not have been so barbarous; Did he threat
To cut thy hand off?

MENTIVOLE
Yes Sir, and his slaves were ready to perform't.

BAPTISTA
What hind'red it?

MENTIVOLE
Only his sons intreaty.

BAPTISTA
Noble youth,
I wish thou wert not of his blood; thy pitty
Gives me a hope thou art not.

MENTIVOLE
You mistake Sir,
The injury that followed from the son,
Was worse than the fathers; he did first disarme
And took from me a Jewel, which I prize
Above my hand or life.

BAPTISTA
Take thy sword from thee?
He stole it like a Thief rather, he could not
I'th' Field deprive thee of it.

MENTIVOLE
He took it from me,
And sent me forth so thin, and so unmade up,
As if I had been a Foot-boy.

BAPTISTA

O my fury!
I must now ask thee forgiveness, that my rashness,
Bred out of too much friendship, did expose thee
To so eminent a danger; which I vow
I will revenge on the whole Family:
All the calamities of my whole life,
My banishment from Genoa, my wifes loss
Compar'd to this indignity, is nothing;
Their Family shall repair't; it shall be to them
Like a plague, when the Dog-star reigns most hot:
An Italian's revenge may pause, but's ne'er forgot.

[Exit.

MENTIVOLE

I would I had conceal'd this from my Father,
For my interest in Clarissa; my care now
Must be to untangle this division,
That our most equal flames may be united;
And from these various and perturbed streames,
Rise, like a sweet Morn, after terrible dreams.—

[Exit.

[Enter **CLARISSA** and **CESARIO**.

CLARISSA

Brother, I am happy in your recovery.

CESARIO

And I Sister, am ever best pleased in your happiness:
But I miss a toy should be on your finger.

CLARISSA

My Ring; this morning when I wash't
I put it off, 'tis in my Window.

CESARIO

Where's your Looking-glass?

CLARISSA

Here, Sir.

CESARIO

'Tis a fair one.

CLARISSA

'Tis pure Chrystal.

CESARIO

Can a Diamond cut in Crystal? let me see,
I'll grave my name in't.

CLARISSA

Oh, you'll spoyl my glass.
Would you not have your brother in your eye?

CESARIO

I had thought he had been Planted in your heart,
Look you, the Diamond cuts quaintly, you are cozen'd,
Your Chrystal is too britle.

CLARISSA

'Tis the Ring
I gave unto Mentivole, sure the same.
You put me to amazement Sir, and horror;
How came you by that Ring?

CESARIO

Does the blood rise?

CLARISSA

Pray Sir resolve me, O for pitty do;
And take from me a trembling at the heart,
That else will kill me: for I too much fear
Nothing but Death could ravish it from his hand
That wore it.

CESARIO

Was it given to Mentivola on that condition?

CLARISSA

Tell me of his health first.
And then I'll tell you any thing.

CESARIO

By my life he's well,
In better health than I am.

CLARISSA

Then it was Sir.

CESARIO

Then shall I ever hate thee, Oh thou false one;

Hast thou a Faith to give unto a friend,
And break it to a brother? Did I not,
By all the tyes of blood importune thee
Never to part with it without my knowledge?
Thou might'st have given it to a Muliter,
And made a contrail with him in a stable,
At as cheap a price of my vengeance: never more
Shall a Womans trust beguile me; You are all
Like Relicks: you may well be look't upon,
But come a Man to'th' handling of you once,
You fall in pieces.

CLARISSA
Dear Sir, I have no way
Look't either beneath reason, or my self,
In my election; there's parity in our blood,
And in our fortunes, antient amity
Betwixt our parents: to which wants nothing,
But the Fruit of blest Marriage between us,
To add to their posterities: nor does now
Any impeachment rise, except the sad
And unexpected quarrel, which divided
So noble, and so excellent a friendship,
Which as I ne'er had Magick to foresee,
So I could not prevent.

CESARIO
Well, you must give me leave
To have a hand in your disposing, I shall,
In the absence of my Father, be your Guardian;
His Suit must pass through my office. Mentivole,
He has too much of my blood already; he has,
And he get's no more of't—
Wherefore weep you Mother?

[Enter **MARIANA**, and a **SAILOR**.

MARIANA
'Tis occasion'd by a sorrow,
Wherein you have a Child's part, and the mainest,
Your Father's dead.

CESARIO
Dead?

MARIANA
There's one can relate the rest.

SAILOR

I can Sir, your Father's drown'd,
Most unfortunately drown'd.

CESARIO

How? In a tempest?

SAILOR

No Sir, in a calm,
Calm as this evening; the Gunner being drunk,
Forgot to fasten the Ordnance to their ports,
When came a sudden gust, which tumbled them
All to the Starboord side, o'erturn'd the Ship,
And sunk her in a moment, some six men
That were upon the deck were sav'd: the rest
Perish'd with your Father.

CLARISSA O my dearest Father—

CESARIO

I pray thee leave us.

MARIANA

I have a sorrow of another nature, equal to the former.

CESARIO

And most commonly they come together.

MARIANA

The Family of the Baptisti
Are grown to faction, and upon distast
Of the injury late offer'd in my house,
Have vow'd a most severe, and fell revenge
'Gainst all our family, but especially
'Gainst you my dear Cæsario.

CESARIO

Let them threat, I am prepar'd to oppose them.

MARIANA

And is your loss then
Of so easie an estimation? What comfort
Have I but in your life, and your late danger
Presents afore me what I am to suffer,
Should you miscarry; therefore I'll advise you
When the Funeral is over, you would travel,
Both to prevent their fury, and wear out th' injury.

CESARIO
No Mother, I will not travel,
So in my absence he may marry my Sister,
I will not travel certain.

MARIANA
O my Cesario,
Whom I respect and love 'bove my own life,
Indeed with a kind of dotage, he shall never
Go forth o' doors, but the contrary faction
Will indanger's life, and then am I most wretched.
I am thinking of a strange prevention,
Which I shall witness with a bleeding eye,
Fondness sometimes is worse than cruelty.—

[Exeunt.

ACTUS TERTIUS

SCÆNA PRIMA

Enter **HOST**, **HOSTESS**, and **BIANCA**.

HOST
Haunted, my house is haunted with goblins. I shall be frighted out of my wits, and set up a sign only to invite Carriers and Foot-posts; scar-crows to keep off the Cavalry, and Gentry of the best rank. I will nail up my doors, and wall up my Girle (wife) like an Anchoress; or she will be ravish before our faces, by rascalls and cacafugo's (wife) cacafugo's.

HOSTESS
These are your In-comes, remember your own proverb, the savor of every gain smelt sweet; thank no body but your self for this trouble.

HOST
No gauling (dear Spouse) no gauling, every days new vexation abates me two inches in the waste, terrible pennance for an Host, Girle, girle, girle, Which of all this gally-maufry of Mans flesh appears tolerable to thy choice; speak shortly, and speak truely: I must and will know, must and will; Hear ye that?

BIANCA
Sir, be not jealous of my care and duty;
I am so far from entertaining thoughts
Of liberty, that much more excellent objects
Than any of such course contents as these are,
Could not betray mine eye to force my heart;
Conceive a wish of any dearer happiness

Than your direction warrant's. I am yours Sir.

HOSTESS
What thinks the Man now? Is not this strange at 13.

HOST
Very good words, there's a tang in e'm, and a sweet one, 'tis musick (wife) and now I come t'ee. Let us a little examine the several conditions of our Paragraphistical suitors. The first, a travelling Tailor, who by the mystery of his Needle and Thimble, hath survey'd the fashions of the French, and English; this Signior Ginger-bread, stitcht up in the shreds of a gaudy outside, sows Linings with his cross-leg'd complement, like an Ape doing tricks over a staffe, cringes, and crouches, and kisses his forefinger.

HOSTESS
Out upon him.

HOST
A second, a lavolteteere, a saltatory, a dancer with a Kit at his Bum, one that, by teaching great Madonnas to foot it, has miraculously purchast a ribanded Wastcote, and four clean pair of socks; a fellow that skips as he walkes, and instead of sensible discourse, vents the curious conceit of some new tune stolen from a Mask, or a bawdy dittie, elevated for the Pole Artick of a Ladies chamber, in that file stands another of your inamoratoes.

HOSTESS
Hang him and his Fiddle together, he never fiddles any child of ours.

HOST
The third, a Mongrel, got by a Switzer on an Italian; this puppy, being left well estated, comes to Florence, that the world may take notice, how impossible it is for experience to alter the course of nature; a fool (wife) and indeed, a Clown turn'd Gallant, seldom or never proves other than a gallant fool, this toy prates to little purpose other than What's a Clock? Shall's go drink? De'e forsooth? And thank ye heartily; I fear no art in him to catch thee, and yet we must be tormented with this buzard amongst the rest.

HOSTESS
'Tis your own folly, forbid him the House.

HOST
The fourth, a Mule-driver, a stubborn and a harsh knave: the fifth a School-Master, a very amorous Pedant, run almost mad with study of Sonnets, and Complements out of old Play-ends, the last an Advocates Clerk, that speaks pure Fustian in Law-terms: excellent Courtiers all, and all as neate as a Magnifio's post new painted, at his entrance to an office; thou shalt have none of 'em. Laugh at 'em, do. I say thou shalt have none of 'em.

BIANCA
Still your command to me shall stand a Law.

HOST

Now they throng like so many horse-coursers at a fair, in clusters about the Man of Art, for Love-powders, ingredients, potions, counsels, postures, complements, philters: the Devil and the—How now? Tumults? Batteries, Noise? ha, get from my sight.

[**CLOWN** cries within.

[Enter **FOROBOSCO**, and **CLOWN**, his head bloody.

CLOWN
Murther me, do, pound me to Mummy, do; see what will come on't.

FOROBOSCO
Dog, leave thy snarling, or I'll cut thy tongue out,
Thou unlickt Bear, dar'st thou yet stand my fury,
My generous rage? yet! by the sulpherous damps
That feed the hungry and incessant darkness,
Which curles around the grim Alastors back,
Mutter again, and with one powerful word,
I'll call an Host up from the Stygian Lakes,
Shall waft thee to the Acherontick fens;
Where choak't with Mists as black as thy impostures,
Thou shalt live still a dying.

CLOWN
Conjure me to the Devil and you can, I live in Hell upon earth already, and you had any mercy, you would not practice upon a kind heart thus.

HOST
You have drawn blood from him Signior, Is his offence unpardonable?

FOROBOSCO
A lump of ignorance, pray speak not for him,
A drowsie grossness, in all Christian Kingdoms,
The mention of my art, my name, my practise,
Merit and Glory hath begot at once
Delight and wonder; I'll not be entreated;
Spare intercession for him,—O thou scorn
Of learning, shame of duty; must thy sloth
Draw my just fame in question? I discharge thee
From my service; see me no more henceforth.

CLOWN
Discharge me! Is that my years wages?
I'll not be so answer'd.

FOROBOSCO
Not Camel? Sirrah I am liberal to thee;
Thou hast thy life, be gone.

CLOWN

Vengeance, sweet vengeance.

FOROBOSCO

De'e mumble?

CLOWN

I'll be reveng'd, monstrously, suddenly, and insatiably; my bulk begins to swell.

FOROBOSCO

Homotolenton,
Pragmatophoros,
Heliostycorax.

CLOWN

Call up your Spirits, I defie 'em; well, I'll have Law for my broken pate, twelve ounces of pure blood;
Troy-weight. In despight of thee my Master, and thy Master the grand Devil himself, vindicta, vindicta.—

[Exit.

HOST

Signior, you are exceeding mov'd.

HOSTESS

Mercy upon us, What terrible words thou talk'st?

FOROBOSCO

A slave, a curr—but be not you afrighted
Young Virgin, 'twere an injury to sweetness:
Should any rough sound draw from your cheeks,
The pretious tincture which makes nature proud
Of her own workmanship.

HOST

Wife, Mark, mark that Wife.

BIANCA

Shake then your anger off Sir.

FOROBOSCO

You command it
Fair one, mine Host and Hostess, with your leaves
I have a motion joyntly to you all.

HOSTESS

An honest one I hope.

HOST
Well put in Wife.

FOROBOSCO
A very necessary one, the Mess
And half of suitors, that attend to usher
Their Loves sir-reverence to your daughter, wait
With one consent, which can best please her eye;
In offering at a Dance, I have provided
Musick. And, 'twill be something I dare promise
Worthy your laughter, Shall they have admittance?

HOST
By any means, for I am perswaded the manner will be so
Ridiculous, that it will confirm the assurance of their
Miserable fooleries, but no longer trouble with 'em here,
Than they are in these May-games.

FOROBOSCO
So I am resolv'd.

HOSTESS
Nor any wise word of senceless love.

FOROBOSCO
Not any; I have charm'd them, Did you see
How they prepar'd themselves? how they stroak up
Their foretops, how they justle for the Looking-glass,
To set their faces by it;

[See they Muster.

You would look for some most impossible antick.

[Enter **TAILOR, DANCER, MULETIER, SCHOOL-MASTER, CLARK**: all with several papers, and present 'em
to **FOROBOSCO**.)

HOST
So, so, so, so, here flutter the nest of Hornets, the hotch-potch of rascallity; now, now, now, now, the
dung-hill of corruption hath yawn'd forth the burthen of abhomination. I am vext, vext to the soul, will
rid my house of this unchristen'd fry, and never open my doors again.

FOROBOSCO
Some other time, I'll give no answer now,
But have preferred your suits, here shew your cunning.
First, every one in order do his honor
To the fair mark you shoot at; courtly, courtly,
Convey your several loves in lively measure:

Come, let us take our seates, some sprightly Musick.

HOST
Dance all and part, 'tis a very necessary farewell.

[Enter **CESARIO.** They all make ridiculous conges to **BIANCA**: rank themselves, and dance in several postures: during the dance, Enter **CESARIO**, and stands off.

HOST
Well done my lusty bloods, precisely well done,
One lusty rouse of Wine, and take leave on all sides.

CESARIO
Thanks for your Revels Gentlemen; accept
This Gold, and drink as freely as you danc'd.

HOST
My noble Lord Cesario, clear the rooms Sirs.

FOROBOSCO
Away. Attend your answers.

[Exeunt **FOROBOSCO**, and those that danc'd.

CESARIO
With your favor Rolando, I would change a word or two with your fair daughter.

HOST
At your Lordships pleasure, come Wife, no muttering, have a care Girle, my love, service, and duty to your good Lordship.

[Exeunt and **WIFE**.

CESARIO
My often visits (sweet Bianca) cannot
But constantly inform thy judgment, wherein
Thy happiness consists, for to steal minutes
From great imployments, to converse with beauty,
Lodg'd in so mean a fortune, to lay by
Consideration of the unequal distance
Between my blood and thine, to shun occasions
Of courtship with the Ladies of the time:
Noble, and fair, only for love to thee,
Must of necessity invite a tenderness;
As low as nature could have stampt a Bondwomans.
To entertain quick motions of rare gratitude
For my uncommon favors.

BIANCA

'Deed my Lord, as far as my simplicity can lead me,
I freely thank your curtesies.

CESARIO

To thank them, is to reward them pretty one.

BIANCA

Then teach me
How I may give them back again; in truth
I never yet receiv'd a pair of Gloves:
A trifling Ring from any that expected
An equall satisfaction, but as willingly
I parted with the guift unto the owner, as he bestow'd it.

CESARIO

But I pour before thee
Such plenties, as it lies not in the ability
Of thy whole kindred, to return proportionable
One for a thousand.

BIANCA

You my Lord conclude
For my instruction, to ingage a debt
Beyond a possibility of paiment,
I ever thought a sin; and therefore justly
Without conceit of scorn, or curious rudeness,
I must refuse your bounty.

CESARIO

Canst thou love?

BIANCA

Love! Is there such a word in any Language
That carries honest sence?

CESARIO

Never dwelt ignorance
In so sweet-shap't a building: love, Bianca,
Is that firm knot which ties two hearts in one:
Shall ours be tied so?

BIANCA

Use a plainer word,
My Lord. In stead of tyes, say marries hearts,
Then I may understand.

CESARIO

Their hearts are married
Whose enterchange of pleasures, and embraces,
Soft kisses, and the privacies of sweets,
Keeps constant league together, when temptation
Of great mens oathes and gifts, shall urge contempt,
Rather than batter resolution, novelty
Of sights, or taste of new delights in wantonness,
Breeds surfeit more than appetite in any
Reserv'd to noble vowes; my excellent Maid,
Live thou but true to me, and my contents,
Mine only, that no partner may partake
The treasure of those sweets thy youth yet glories in,
And I will raise thy lowness to abundance
Of all varieties, and more triumph
In such a Mistris, than great Princes doating
On truth-betraying Wives.

BIANCA
Thus to yield up then
The cottage of my virtue, to be swallow'd
By some hard-neighbouring Landlord, such as you are,
Is in effect to love, a Lord so vicious!
O where shall innocence find some poor dwelling,
Free from temptations tyranny.

CESARIO
Nay prethee.

BIANCA
Gay clothes, high feeding, easie beds of lust,
Change of unseemly sights; with base discourse,
Draw curses on your Pallaces; for my part,
This I will be confirm'd in, I will eate
The bread of labour, know no other rest
Than what is earn'd from honest pains, ere once more
Lend ear to your vile toyles; Sir, would you were
As noble in desires, as I could be in knowing virtue.
Pray do not afflict a poor soul thus.

CESARIO
I swear—to me?—

[**BIANCA** steals off.

[Enter a **GENTLEMAN**.

GENTLEMAN
The Duke my Lord commands your speedy presence

For answering agrievances lately urg'd
Against you by your Mother?

CESARIO
By my Mother.

GENTLEMAN
The Court is near on sitting.

CESARIO
I wait on it Sir.—

[Exeunt.

[Enter **DUKE of FLORENCE**, **MAGISTRATE**, **SECRETARY**, **BAPTISTA**, **ATTENDANTS**, **MENTIVOLE**: they sit.
MENTIVOLE stands by.

DUKE of FLORENCE
What waste of blood, what tumults, what divisions,
What outrages, what uprores in a State,
Factions, though issuing from mean springs at first,
Have (not restrain'd) flowed to, the sad example
At Rome, between the Ursins and Columni's:
Nay, here at home, in Florence, 'twixt the Neers
And the Bianchi, can too mainly witness.
I sit not at the Helm (my Lords) of Sovereignty
Deputed Pilot for the Common-wealth,
To sleep while others steere (as their wild fancies
Shall counsel) by the compass of disorders.
Baptista, This short Preface is directed
Chiefly to you, the petty brawls and quarrels
Late urg'd betwixt th' Alberti and your family;
Must, yes, and shall, like tender unknit joynts,
Fasten again together of themselves:
Or like an angry surgeon, we will use
The roughness of our justice, to cut off
The stubborn rancour of the limbes offending.

BAPTISTA
Most gracious Florence.

DUKE of FLORENCE
Our command was signified,
That neither of the followers of each party
Should appear here with weapons.

BAPTISTA
'Tis obey'd Sir, on my side.

DUKE of FLORENCE
We must leave the general cause
Of State employments, to give ear to brawls
Of some particular grudges, pollitick government
For tutor'd Princes, but no more henceforth.

[Enter **MARIANA**, and **CLARISSA** at one door, **CESARIO** at the other.

Our frown shall check presumption, not our clemency.

MARIANA
All blessings due to unpartial Princes,
Crown Florence with eternity of happiness.

CESARIO
If double Prayers can double blessings (great Sir)
Mine joyn for your prosperity with my Mothers.

DUKE of FLORENCE
Rise both; now briefly (Lady) without circumstance
Deliver those agrievances, which lately
Your importunity possest our Counsel,
Were fit for audience, wherein you petition'd,
You might be heard without an Advocate,
Which boon you find is granted.

MARIANA
Though divided.
I stand between the Laws of truth and modesty,
Yet let my griefs have vent: Yet the clearness
Of strange necessity requires obedience
To nature and your Mercy, in my weeds
Of mourning, emblems of too dear misfortunes,
Badges of griefs, and Widdowhood, the burthen
Of my charg'd soul, must be laid down before you;
Wherein, if strict opinion cancel shame,
My frailty is my plea;
Stand forth young Man,
And hear a story that will strike all reason
Into amazement.

CESARIO
I attend.

MARIANA
Alberto (peace dwell upon his ashes) still the husband
Of my remembrance and unchanging vowes,

Has, by his death, left to his heir possession
Of fair revenew, which this young man claimes
As his inheritance. I urg'd him gently,
Friendly, and privately, to grant a partage
Of this estate to her who ownes it all,
This his supposed Sister.

BAPTISTA
How supposed?

CESARIO
Pray Madam recollect your self.

MARIANA
The relish
Of a strange truth begins to work like Physick
Already: I have bitterness to mingle
With these preparatives, so deadly loathsome;
It will quite choak digestion; shortly hear it
Cesario, for I dare not rob unjustly
The poor soul of his name; this, this Cesario
Neither for Father had Alberto, me
For Mother, nor Clarissa for his Sister.

CLARISSA
Mother, O Mother.

MENTIVOLE
I am in a Dream sure.

DUKE of FLORENCE
No interruptions. Lady on.

MARIANA
Mistake not,
Great Duke of Tuscany, or the beginning
Or process of this novelty; my husband
The now deceas'd Alberto, from his youth
In-ur'd to an impatiency, and roughness
Of disposition, when not many months
After our Marriage were worn out, repin'd
At the unfruitful barrenness of youth,
Which, as he pleas'd to terme it, cut our hopes off
From blessing of some issue; to prevent it
I grew ambitious of no fairer honor
Than to preserve his love, and as occasions
Still call'd him from me, studied in his absence
How I might frame his welcome home with comfort.

At last I fain'd my self with Child; the Message
Of freedome, or relief, to one half starv'd
In prison, is not utter'd with such greediness
Of expectation, and delight, as this was
To my much affected Lord; his care, his goodness;
(Pardon me that I use the word) exceeded
All former fears, the hour of my deliverance
As I pretended, drawing near, I fashion'd
My birth-rights at a Country Garden-house,
Where then my Faulk'ners Wife was brought a bed
Of this Cesario; him I own'd for mine;
Presented him unto a joyful Father.

DUKE of FLORENCE
Can you prove this true?

MARIANA
Proofs I have most evident;
But oh the curse of my impatiency; shortly,
E'r three new Moons had spent their borrow'd Lights,
I grew with Child indeed, so just is Heaven,
The issue of which burthen was this Daughter;
Judge now most gracious Prince, my Lords and you,
What combats then, and since, I have indur'd,
Between a Mothers piety, and weakness
Of a Soul trembling Wife; to have reveal'd
This secret to Alberto, had been danger
Of ruin to my fame, besides the conflict
Of his distractions; now to have supprest it,
Were to defeat my Child, my only Child,
Of her most lawful honors, and inheritance.
Cæsario, th'art a Man still, Education
Hath moulded thee a Gentleman, continue so;
Let not this fall from greatness sink thee lower
Than worthy thoughts may warrant, yet disclaim
All interest in Alberto's blood, thou hast not
One drop of his or mine.

DUKE of FLORENCE
Produce your witness.

MARIANA
The Faulconers Wife his Mother,
And such women as waited then upon me,
Sworn to the privacy of this great secret.

DUKE of FLORENCE
Give them all their Oaths.

CESARIO

O let me crave forbearance, gracious Sir,
Vouchsafe me hearing.

DUKE of FLORENCE

Speak Cæsario.

CESARIO

Thus long
I have stood silent, and with no unwillingness,
Attended the relation of my fall,
From a fair expectation; what I fear'd
(Since the first syllable this Lady utter'd
Of my not being hers) benevolent Fates
Have eas'd me off; for to be basely born,
If not base-born, detracts not from the bounty
Of natures freedom, or an honest birth.
Nobility claim'd by the right of blood,
Shewes chiefly, that our Ancestors desir'd
What we inherit; but that Man whose actions
Purchase a real merit to himself,
And rancks him in the file of praise and honor,
Creates his own advancement; let me want
The fuel which best feeds the fires of greatness,
Lordly possessions, yet shall still my gratitude
By some attempts, of mention not unworthy,
Endeavour to return a fit acquittance
To that large debt I owe your favours (Madam)
And great Alberto's memory and goodness;
O that I could as gently shake off passion
For the loss of that great brave Man, as I can shake off
Remembrance of that once I was reputed;
I have not much to say, this Princely presence
Needs not too strictly to examine farther
The truth of this acknowledgment; a Mother
Dares never disavow her only son,
And any woman must come short of Piety,
That can, or dis-inherit her own issue,
Or fears the voice of rumor for a stranger.
Madam, you have confest, my Father was
A servant to your Lord and you: by interest
Of being his son, I cannot but claim justly
The honor of continuing still my service
To you and yours; which granted, I beg leave
I may for this time be dismist.

DUKE of FLORENCE

Bold spirit.

BAPTISTA
I love thee now with pitty.

DUKE of FLORENCE
Go not yet—
A sudden tempest that might shake a rock,
Yet he stands firm against it; much it moves me,
He, not Alberto's son, and she a Widdow,
And she a Widdow,—Lords your ear.

OMNES
Your pleasure.—

[Whispers.

DUKE of FLORENCE
So, Lady, what you have avouch'd is truth.

MARIANA
Truth only, gracious Sir.

DUKE of FLORENCE
Hear then our Sentence.
Since from his cradle you have fed and foster'd
Cæsario as your Son, and train'd him up
To hopes of greatness; which now in a moment
You utterly again have ruin'd, this way
We with our Counsel are resolv'd, you being
A Widdow, shall accept him for a husband.

MARIANA
Husband to me, Sir?

DUKE of FLORENCE
'Tis in us to raise him
To honors, and his vertues will deserve 'em.

MARIANA
But Sir, 'tis in no Prince, nor his Prerogative,
To force a Womans choice against her heart.

DUKE of FLORENCE
True, if then you appeale to higher Justice,
Our Doom includes this clause upon refusal,
Out of your Lords revenues shall Cæsario
Assure to any, whom he takes for Wife,

The inheritance of three parts; the less remainer
Is dowry large enough to marry a daughter;
And we, by our Prerogative, which you question,
Will publickly adopt him into th'name
Of your deceas'd Alberto, that the memory
Of so approv'd a Peer may live in him
That can preserve his memory; 'less you find out
Some other means, which may as amply satisfie
His wrong, our Sentence stands irrevocable:
What think you Lords?

OMNES
The Duke is just and honorable.

BAPTISTA
Let me embrace Cæsario, henceforth ever
I vow a constant friendship.

MENTIVOLE
I remit all former difference.

CESARIO
I am too poor
In words to thank this Justice. Madam, always
My studies shall be love to you, and duty.

DUKE of FLORENCE
Replies we admit none. Cæsario wait on us.

[Exeunt. Manent, **MENTIVOLE, BAPTISTA, MARIANA, CLARISSA.**

BAPTISTA
Mentivole.

MENTIVOLE
My Lord.

BAPTISTA
Look on Clarissa, she's noble, rich, young, fair.

MENTIVOLE
My Lord, and virtuous.

BAPTISTA
Mentivole and virtuous.—Madam.

MARIANA
Tyranny of Justice, I shall live reports derision,

That am compell'd to exchange a graceful Widdowhood
For a continual Martyrdome in Marriage,
With one so much beneath me.

BAPTISTA
I'll plead for ye
Boldly and constantly, let your daughter only
Admit my son her servant, at next visit,
Madam, I'll be a messenger of comfort.
Mentivole, be confident and earnest.

[Exit.

MARIANA
Married again, to him too! better 'thad been
The young Man should have still retain'd the honors
Of old Alberto's son, than I the shame
Of making him successor of his bed; I was too blame.

MENTIVOLE
Indeed without offence,
Madam I think you were.

CLARISSA
You urge it fairly, and like a worthy friend.

MARIANA
Can you say any thing
In commendation of a Mushroom withered
As soon as started up?

MENTIVOLE
You scorn an Innocent
Of noble growth, for whiles your husband liv'd
I have heard you boast Cesario in all actions
Gave matter of report of Imitation,
Wonder and envy; let not discontinuance
Of some few days estrange a sweet opinion
Of virtue, chiefly when, in such extremity,
Your pitty not contempt will argue goodness.

MARIANA
O Sir.

CLARISSA
If you would use a thriving courtship,
You cannot utter a more powerfull language
That I shall listen to with greater greediness

Than th' argument you prosecute; this speaks you
A man compleat and excellent.

MENTIVOLE
I speak not, they are his own deserts.

MARIANA
Good Sir forbear,
I am now fully sensible of running
Into a violent Lethargy, whose deadliness
Locks up all reason, I shall never henceforth
Remember my past happiness.

MENTIVOLE
These clouds may be disperst.

MARIANA
I fear continuall night
Will over-shroud me, yet poor youth his trespass
Lies in his fortune, not the cruelty
Of the Duke's sentence.

CLARISSA
I dare think it does.

MARIANA
If all fail I will learn thee to conquer
Adversity with sufferance.

MENTIVOLE
You resolve Nobly.

[Exeunt.

ACTUS QUARTUS

SCÆNA PRIMA

Enter **CESARIO** and a **SERVANT**.

CESARIO
Let any friend have entrance.

SERVANT
Sir a'shall.

CESARIO
Any, I except none.

SERVANT
We know, your mind Sir.

[Exit.

CESARIO
Pleasures admit no bounds.
I am pitcht so high
To such a growth of full prosperities
That to conceal my fortunes were an injury
To gratefulness, and those more liberall favours
By whom my glories prosper. He that flowes
In gracious and swolne tydes of best abundance,
Yet will be Ignorant of his own fortunes,
Deserves to live contemn'd, and dye forgotten;
The harvest of my hopes is now already
Ripen'd and gather'd, I can fatten youth
With choice of plenty, and supplies of comforts,
My fate springs in my own hand, and I'll use it.

[Enter **TWO SERVANTS** and **BIANCA**.

1ST SERVANT
'Tis my place.

2ND SERVANT
Yours? here fair one, I'll aquaint my Lord.

1ST SERVANT
He's here, go to him boldly.

2ND SERVANT
Please you to let him understand how readily
I waited on your errand?

1ST SERVANT
Saucy fellow, you must excuse his breeding.

CESARIO
What's the matter?
Bianca, my Bianca, to your offices.

[Exit **SERVANT**.

This visit (Sweet) from thee (my pretty dear)

By how much more 'twas unexpected, comes
So much the more timely: witness this free welcome,
What ere occasion led thee.

BIANCA
You must guess Sir,
Yet indeed 'tis a rare one.

CESARIO
Prethee speak it, my honest virtuous maid.

BIANCA
Sir I have heard
Of your misfortunes, and I cannot tell you
Whether I have more cause of joy or sadness,
To know they are a truth.

CESARIO
What truth Bianca? misfortunes, how, wherein?

BIANCA
You are disclaym'd
For being the Lord Alberto's Son, and publickly
Acknowledg'd of as mean a birth as mine is,
It cannot chuse but greive ye.

CESARIO
Greive me? Ha ha ha ha? Is this all?

BIANCA
This all?

CESARIO
Thou art sorry for't
I warrant thee: alas good soul, Bianca,
That which thou call'st misfortune is my happiness,
My happiness Bianca.

BIANCA
If you love me, it may prove mine too.

CESARIO
May it? I will love thee.
My good, good maid,
If that can make thee happy,
Better and better love thee.

BIANCA

Without breach then
Of modesty I come to claime the Interest
Your protestations, both by vows and letters,
Have made me owner of: from the first hour
I saw you, I confess I wisht I had been
Or not so much below your rank and greatness,
Or not so much above those humble flames
That should have warm'd my bosome with a temperate
Equality of desires in equal fortunes.
Still as you utter'd Language of affection,
I courted time to pass more slowly on
That I might turn more fool to lend attention
To what I durst not credit, nor yet hope for:
Yet still as more I heard, I wisht to hear more.

CESARIO
Didst thou introth wench?

BIANCA
Willingly betraid
My self to hopeless bondage.

CESARIO
A good girl,
I thought I should not miss
What ere thy answer was.

BIANCA
But as I am a maid Sir, and I'faith
You may believe me, for I am a maid,
So dearly I respected both your fame
And quality, that I would first have perisht
In my sick thoughts than ere have given consent
To have undone your fortunes by inviting
A marriage with so mean an one as I am.
I should have dyed sure, and no creature known
The sickness that had kill'd me.

CESARIO
Pretty heart, good Soul, alas, alas.

BIANCA
Now since I know
There is no difference 'twixt your birth and mine,
Not much 'twixt our estates, if any be,
The advantage is on my side, I come willingly
To tender you the first fruits of my heart,
And am content t'accept you for my husband,

Now when you are at lowest.

CESARIO
For a husband?
Speak sadly, dost thou mean so?

BIANCA
In good deed Sir,
'Tis pure love makes this proffer.

CESARIO
I believe thee,
What counsail urg'd thee on, tell me, thy Father
My worshipfull smug Host? wast not he wench?
Or mother Hostess? ha?

BIANCA
D'ee mock my parentage?
I doe not scorn yours.
Mean folks are as worthy
To be well spoken of if they deserve well,
As some whose onely fame lies in their blood,
O y'are a proud poor man: all your oaths falshood,
Your vows deceit, your letters forg'd, and wicked.

CESARIO
Thou'dst be my wife, I dare swear.

BIANCA
Had your heart,
Your hand and tongue been twins, you had reputed
This courtesy a benefit.

CESARIO
Simplicity,
How prettily thou mov'st me! why Bianca,
Report has coz'ned thee, I am not fallen
From my expected honors, or possessions,
Though from the hope of birthright.

BIANCA
Are you not?
Then I am lost again, I have a suit too;
You'll grant it if you be a good man.

CESARIO
Any thing.

BIANCA

Pray doe not talk of ought what I have said t'ee.

CESARIO

As I wish health I will not.

BIANCA

Pitty me, but never love me more.

CESARIO

Nay now y'are cruell,
Why all these tears?—Thou shalt not go.

BIANCA

I'll pray for ye
That you may have a virtuous wife, a fair one,
And when I am dead—

CESARIO

Fy, fy.

BIANCA

Think on me sometimes,
With mercy for this trespass.

CESARIO

Let us kiss
At parting as at coming.

BIANCA

This I have
As a free dower to a virgins grave,
All goodness dwell with ye.—

[Exit.

CESARIO

Harmeless Bianca! unskill'd;
What hansome toyes are maids to play with!

[Enter **MARIANA** and **CLARISSA**.

How innocent! But I have other thoughts
Of nobler meditation.—my felicity,
Thou commest as I could wish, lend me a lip
Soft as melting as when old Alberto
After his first nights triall taking farewell
Of thy youth's conquest tasted.

MARIANA
You are uncivill.

CESARIO
I will be Lord of my own pleasures, Madam
Y'are mine, mine freely,
Come, no whimpering henceforth
New con the lessons of loves best experience,
That our delights may meet in equal measure
Of resolutions and desires; this sulleness
Is scurvy, I like it not.

MARIANA
Be modest.
And do not learn Cesario how to prostitute
The riot of thy hopes to common folly;
Take a sad womans word, how ere thou doat'st
Upon the present graces of thy greatnes.
Yea I am not falen so below my constancy
To virtue, nor the care which I once tend'red
For thy behoof that I prefer a sentence
Of cruelty before my honor.

CESARIO
Honor!

MARIANA
Hear me, thou seest this girl! now the comfort
Of my last days. She is the onely pledge
Of a bed truely noble: shee had a father
(I need not speak him more than thou remembrest)
Whom to dishonor by a meaner choice,
Were injury and infamy.

CLARISSATo goodnes,
To time and virtuous mention.

MARIANA
I have vow'd,
Observe me now Cesario, that how ere
I may be forc'd to marry, yet no tyranny,
Persuasions, flattery, guifts, intreats, or tortures,
Shall draw me to a second bed.

CLARISSA
Tis just too.

MARIANA

Yes and 'tis just Clarissa. I allow
The Duke's late sentence, am resolv'd young man
To be thy wife, but when the ceremony
Of marriage is perform'd, in life I will be,
Though not in name, a widdow.

CESARIO

Pray a word t'ee,
Shall I in earnest never be your bedfellow?

MARIANA

Never, O never; and 'tis for your good too.

CESARIO

Prove that.

MARIANA

Alas too many years are numbred
In my account to entertain the benefit
Which youth in thee Cesario, and ability
Might hope for and require, it were Injustice
To rob a gentleman deserving memory
Of Issue to preserve it.

CESARIO

No more herein,
You are an excellent pattern of true piety,
Let me now turn your advocate. Pray look into
The order of the Duke. Injoyn'd, admit
I satisfie the sentence without mariage
With you, how then?

MARIANA

Cesario.

CESARIO

If I know
How to acquit your fears, yet keep th'injunction
In every clause whole and entire, your charity
Will call me still your servant.

MARIANA

Still my son.

CESARIO

Right Madam, now you have it, still your son.
The Genius of your blessings hath instructed

Your tongue oraculously, we will forget
How once I and Clarissa enterchang'd
The tyes of brother and of sister, henceforth
New stile us man and wife.

CLARISSA
By what authority?

CESARIO
Heavens great appointment, yet in all my dotage
On thy perfections, when I thought Clarissa
We had been pledges of one womb, no lose
No wanton heat of youth, desir'd to claime
Priority in thy affections, other
Than nature might commend. Chastly I tend'red
Thy welfare as a brother ought; but since
Our bloods are strangers, let our hearts contract
A long life-lasting unity, for this way
The sentence is to be observ'd or no way.

MARIANA
Then no way.

CESARIO
I expected other answer Madam from you.

MARIANA
No, every age shall curse me,
The monster, and the prodigie of nature,
Horrors beyond extremity.

CLARISSA
Pray mother confine the violence of greif.

CESARIO
Yes mother, pray do.

MARIANA
Thus some catch at a matrons honor
By flying lust to plot Incestuous witchcrafts.
More terrible than whoredomes; cruell mercy!
When to preserve the body from a death
The soul is strangled.

CESARIO
This is more than passion,
It comes near to distraction.

MARIANA
I am quieted.
Cesario, thou mayest tell the Duke securely
Alberto's titles, honors and revenues,
The Duke may give away, enjoy them thou.
Clarissas birthright, Marianas dower
Thou shalt be Lord of; turn us to the world
Unpittied and unfriended, yet my bed
Thou never sleep'st in; as for her; she hears me,
If she as much as in a thought consent;
That thou may'st call her wife, a Mothers curse
Shall never leave her.

CLARISSA
As a brother once
I lov'd you, as a noble friend yet honor ye,
But for a husband sir, I dare not own you,
My faith is given already.

CESARIO
To a Villain, I'll cut his throat.

MARIANA
Why this is more than passion!
It comes near a distraction.

CLARISSA
Call to mind Sir.
How much you have abated of that goodness
Which once reign'd in ye, they appear'd so lovely
That such as friendship led to observation

[Enter **BAPTISTA** and **MENTIVOLE**.

Courted the great example.

CESARIO
Left, and flatter'd into a broad derision?

MARIANA
Why d'ee think so?
My Lord Baptista, is your Son grown cold
In hasting on the marriage, which his vows
Have seal'd to my wrong'd daughter?

BAPTISTA
We come Lady, to consummate the contract.

CESARIO
With Mentivole? is he the man?

MENTIVOLE
Clarissas, troth and mine,
Cesario, are recorded in a character
So plain and certain, that except the hand
Of heaven, which writ it first, would blot it out again,
No humane power can raze it.

CESARIO
But say you so too young Lady?

CLARISSA
I should else betray
My heart to falshood, and my tongue to perjury.

CESARIO
Madam, you know the sentence.

BAPTISTA
From the Duke,
I have particular comforts which require
A private eare.

MARIANA
I shall approve it gladly
We are resolv'd Cesario.

BAPTISTA
Be not insolent upon a Princes favor.

CLARISSA
Loose no glory,
Your younger years have purchast.

MENTIVOLE
And deserved too, y'have many worthy freinds.

BAPTISTA
Preserve and use them.

[Exeunt. Manet **CESARIO**.

CESARIO
Good, very good, why here's a complement
Of mirth in desperation, I could curse
My fate: O with what speed men tumble down

From hopes that soar too high. Bianca now
May scorn me justly too, Clarissa married,
Alberto's widdow resolute, Bianca
Refus'd, and I forsaken: let me study,
I can but die a Batchelor that's the worst on't.

[Exit.

[Enter **HOST, TAILOR, MULETIER, DANCER, PEDANT, COXCOMBE**.

HOST
Come Gentlemen,
This is the day that our great artist hath
Promis'd to give all your severall suits satisfaction.

DANCER
Is he stirring?

HOST
He hath been at his book these two hours.

PEDANT
He's a rare Physitian.

HOST
Why I'll tell you,
Were Paracelsus the German now
Living, he'd take up his single rapier against his
Terrible long sword, he makes it a matter of nothing
To cure the gout, sore eyes he takes out as familiarly,
Washes them, and puts them in again,
As you'd blanch almonds.

TAILOR
They say he can make gold.

HOST
I, I, he learnt it of Kelly in Germanny.
There's not a Chymist
In christendome can goe beyond him for multiplying.

PEDANT
Take heed then;
He get not up your daughters belly my Host.

HOST
You are a merry Gentleman
And the man of art will love you the better.

DANCER
Does he love mirth and crotchets?

HOST
O he's the most courteous Physitian,
You may drink or drab in's company freely,
The better he knows how your disease grows,
The better he knows how to cure it.

DANCER
But I wonder my Host
He has no more resort of Ladyes to him.

HOST
Why Sir?

DANCER
O divers of them have great beleif in conjurers:
Lechery is a great help to the quality.

HOST
He's scarce known to be in town yet,
Ere long we shall have 'em come
Hurrying hither in Fetherbeds.

DANCER
How? bedridden?

HOST
No sir, in fetherbeds that move upon 4 wheels in
Spanish caroches.

PEDANT
Pray accquaint him we give attendance.

HOST
I shall gentlemen; I would fain be rid
Of these rascalls, but that they raise profit
To my wine cellar.
When I have made use of them sufficiently,
I will intreat the conjurer to tye crackers to their tails,
And send them packing.

[Enter **FOROBOSCO** as in his Study. Reading a paper.

FOROBOSCO
Come hither mine Host, look here.

FOROBOSCO
That the devill himself
Might not go beyond you.

DANCER
You are i'th' right Sir.

FOROBOSCO
And so your mony for your purchase
Might come in again within a 12 month.

DANCER
I would be a Graduate sir, no freshman.

FOROBOSCO
Here's my hand sir,
I will make you dissemble so methodically,
As if the divell should be sent from the great Turk,
In the shape of an Embassador
To set all the Christian princes at variance.

DANCER
I cannot with any modesty desire any more.
There's your mony sir.

FOROBOSCO
For the art of dissembling.

COXCOMBE
My suit sir will be news to you when I tell it.

FOROBOSCO
Pray on.

COXCOMBE
I would set up a press here in Italy,
To write all the Corantos for Christendome.

FOROBOSCO
That's news indeed,
And how would you imploy me in't?

COXCOMBE
Marry sir, from you
I would gain my intelligence.

FOROBOSCO

HOST
What's that?

FOROBOSCO
A challenge from my man.

HOST
For breaking's pate?

FOROBOSCO
He writes here if I meet him not
I'th' Feild within this half hour,
I shall hear more from him.

HOST
O sir, minde your profit,
Ne'er think of the rascall, here are the gentlemen.

FOROBOSCO
'Morrow my worthy clients,
What are you all prepar'd of your questions;
That I may give my resolution upon them?

OMNES
We are Sir.

PEDANT
And have brought our mony.

FOROBOSCO
Each then in order,
And differ not for precedency.

DANCER
I am buying of an office Sir,
And to that purpose I would fain learn
To dissemble cunningly.

FOROBOSCO
Doe you come to me for that? you should rather
Have gone to a cunning woman.

DANCER
I sir but their Instructions are but like women,
Pretty well but not to the depth, as I'd have it:
You are a conjurer, the devils Master,
And I would learn it from you so exactly.

I conceive you, you would have me furnish you
With a spirit to informe you.

COXCOMBE
But as quiet a Divell as the woman,
The first day and a half after she's married,
I can by no means indure a terrible one.

FOROBOSCO
No, no, I'll qualifie him,
He shall not fright you,
It shall be the ghost of some lying Stationer,
A Spirit shall look as if butter would not melt in his mouth.
A new Mercurius Gallo-belgicus.

COXCOMBE
O there was a captain was rare at it.

FOROBOSCO
Ne'er thinke of him,
Though that captain writ a full hand gallop,
And wasted indeed more harmless paper than
Ever did laxative Physick,
Yet will I make you to out-scribble him,
And set down what you please,
The world shall better believe you.

COXCOMBE
Worthy sir I thank you, there's mony.

FOROBOSCO
A new office
For writing pragmaticall Curranto's.

PEDANT
I am a school-master sir,
And would fain conferre with you
About erecting four new sects of religion at Amsterdam.

FOROBOSCO
What the Divell should
New sects of religion doe there?

PEDANT
I assure you I would get
A great deal of money by it.

FOROBOSCO

And what are the four new sects
Of religion you would plant there?

PEDANT
Why that's it I come about sir,
'Tis a Divel of your raising must invent 'em,
I confess I am too weak to compass it.

FOROBOSCO
So sir, then you make it a matter of no difficulty
To have them tolerated.

PEDANT
Trouble not your self for that,
Let but your Divel set them a foot once.
I have Weavers, and Ginger-bread makers,
And mighty Aquavitæ-men, shall set them a going.

FOROBOSCO
This is somewhat difficult,
And will aske some conference with the divell.

PEDANT
Take your own leasure sir,
I have another business too, because I mean
To leave Italy, and bury my self in those neather parts
Of the low countries.

FOROBOSCO
What's that sir.

PEDANT
Marry I would fain make 9 dayes to the week,
for the more ample benefit of the captain.

FOROBOSCO
You have a shrewd pate sir.

PEDANT
But how this might be compass'd?

FOROBOSCO
Compass'd easily; tis but making
A new Almanack, and dividing the compass
Of the year into larger penny-worths,
As a Chandler with his compass makes
A Geometrick proportion of the Holland cheese
He retailes by stivers.

But for getting of it licenc'd?

PEDANT
Trouble not your self with that sir,
There's your mony.

FOROBOSCO
For four new sects of religions,
And 9 dayes to the week.

PEDANT
To be brought in at general pay-dayes,
Write I beseech you.

FOROBOSCO
At generall pay-dayes.

TAILOR
I am by profession a Taylor,
You have heard of me.

FOROBOSCO
Yes sir, and will not steal from you
The least part of that commendation I have heard utter'd.

TAILOR
I take measure of your worth sir,
And because I will not afflict you with any large bill
Of circumstances, I will snip off particulars.
I would fain invent some strange
And exquisite new fashions.

FOROBOSCO
Are you not travel'd sir.

TAILOR
Yes sir, but have observ'd all we can see
Or invent, are but old ones with new names to'em,
Now I would some way or other grow more curious.

FOROBOSCO
Let me see; to devise new fashions—
Were you never in the Moon?

TAILOR
In the Moon tavern! yes sir, often.

FOROBOSCO

No, I do mean in the new world,
In the world that's in the Moon yonder.

TAILOR
How? a new world 'ith' moon?

FOROBOSCO
Yes I assure you.

TAILOR
And peopled?

FOROBOSCO
O most fantastically peopled.

TAILOR
Nay certain then there's work for taylors?

FOROBOSCO
That there is I assure you.

TAILOR
Yet I have talked with a Scotch taylor
That never discover'd so much to me,
Though he has travell'd far, and was a pedlar in Poland.

FOROBOSCO
That was out of his way,
This lies beyond China:
You would study new fashions you say?
Take my councell, make a voyage,
And discover that new world.

TAILOR
Shall I be a moon-man?

FOROBOSCO
I am of opinion, the people of that world
(If they be like the nature of that climate they live in)
Do vary the fashion of their cloaths oftener than any
Quick-silver'd nation in Europe.

TAILOR
Not unlikely, but what should that be we call
The man in the moon then?

FOROBOSCO
Why 'tis nothing but an Englishman

That stands there stark naked,
With a pair of sheers in one hand,
And a great bundle of broad cloath in the other
(Which resembles the bush of thorns)
Cutting out of new fashions.

TAILOR
I have heard somewhat like this,
But how shall I get thither?

FOROBOSCO
I'll make a new compass shall direct you.

TAILOR
Certain?

FOROBOSCO
Count me else for no man of direction.

TAILOR
There's 20 duckats in hand, at my return
I'll give you a 100.

FOROBOSCO
A new voyage to discover new fashions.

MULETIER
I have been a traveller too sir,
That have shewed strange beasts in Christendome,
And got money by them, but I find the trade to decay.
Your Camelion, or East-Indian hedg-hog
Gets very little mony, and your Elephant devours
So much bread, brings in so little profit,
His keeper were better every morning
Cram 15 Taylors with white manchet:
I would have some new spectacle,
And one that might be more attractive.

FOROBOSCO
Let me see, were you ever in Spain?

MULETIER
Not yet Sir.

FOROBOSCO
I would have you go to Madrill, and against some great festivall, when the court lies there, provide a
great and spacious English Oxe, and rost him whole, with a pudding in's bely; that would be the eighth
wonder of the world in those parts I assure you.

MULETIER

A rare project without question.

FOROBOSCO

Goe beyond all their garlike olle padridoes, though you sod one in Garguentuas couldron, bring in more money, then all the monsters of Affrick.

HOST

Good Sir do your best for him; he's of my acquaintance, and one if ye knew him—

FOROBOSCO

What is he?

HOST

He was once a man of infinite letters.

FOROBOSCO

A Scholar?

HOST

No sir, a packet carrier, which is alwaies a man of many letters, you know: then he was Mule-driver, now he's a gentleman, and feeds monsters.

FOROBOSCO

A most ungratefull calling.

MULETIER

There's money for your direction; the price of the Oxe
Sir?

FOROBOSCO

A hundred French crowns, for it must be a Lincolne-shire Oxe, and a prime one: For a rare and monstrous spectacle, to be seen at Madrill.

[Enter **CLOWN**, **HOSTESS**, and **BIANCA**.

HOSTESS

Pray forbear sir, we shall have a new quarrell.

CLOWN

You durst not meet me 'ith field, I am therefore come to spoyl your market.

FOROBOSCO

What's the newes with you sir.

CLOWN

Gentlemen, you that come hither to be most abominably cheated, listen, and be as wise as your planet will suffer you, keep your mony, be not gul'd, be not laught at.

PEDANT
What means this? would I had my mony again in my pocket.

HOST
The fellow is full of malice, do not mind him.

CLOWN
This profest cheating rogue was my master, and I confess my self a more preternotorious rogue than himself, in so long keeping his villainous counsell.

FOROBOSCO
Come, come, I will not hear you.

CLOWN
No couz'ner, thou wouldest not hear me, I do but dare thee to suffer me to speak, and then thou and all thy divells spit fire, and spout Aqua fortis.

FOROBOSCO
Speak on, I freely permit thee.

CLOWN
Why then know all you simple animals, you whose purses are ready to cast the calf; if they have not cast it already, if you give any credit to this jugling rascal, you are worse than simple widgins, and will be drawn into the net by this decoy duck, this tame cheater.

FOROBOSCO
Ha, ha, ha, pray mark him.

CLOWN
He does profess Physicke, and counjuring; for his Physick; he has but two medicines for all manner of diseases; when he was i'th' low countryes, he us'd nothing but butter'd beer, colour'd with Allegant, for all kind of maladies, and that he called his catholick med'cine; sure the Dutch smelt out it was butter'd beer, else they would never have endur'd it for the names sake: then does he minister a grated Dogs turd instead of Rubarb, many times of Unicornes horn, which working strongly with the conceit of the Patient, would make them bescummer to the height of a mighty purgation.

FOROBOSCO
The rogue has studied this invective.

CLOWN
Now for his conjuring, the witches of Lapland are the divells chare-women to him, for they will sell a man a wind to some purpose; he sells wind, and tells you fortie lyes over and over.

HOSTESS
I thought what we should find of him.

HOST
Hold your prating, be not you an heretick.

CLOWN
Conjure! I'll tell you, all the divells names he calls upon are but fustion names, gather'd out of welch heraldry; in breif, he is a rogue of six reprieves, four pardons of course, thrice pilloried, twice sung Lacrymæ to the Virginalls of a carts tail, h'as five times been in the Gallies, and will never truely run himself out of breath, till he comes to the gallowes.

FOROBOSCO
You have heard worthy gentlemen, what this lying, detracting rascall has vomited.

TAILOR
Yes certain, but we have a better trust in you, for you have ta'en our money.

FOROBOSCO
I have so, truth is he was my servant, and for some chastisement I gave him, he does practise thus upon me; speak truely sirra, are you certain I cannot conjure?

CLOWN
Conjure! ha, ha, ha.

FOROBOSCO
Nay, nay, but be very sure of it.

CLOWN
Sure of it? why I'll make a bargain with thee, before all these gentlemen, use all thy art, all thy roguery, and make me do any thing before al this company I have not a mind to, I'll first give thee leave to claime me for thy bond slave, and when thou hast done hang me.

FOROBOSCO
'Tis a match, sirra, I'll make you caper i'th' air presently.

CLOWN
I have too solid a body, and my belief is like a Puritans on Good-Friday, too high fed with capon.

FOROBOSCO
I will first send thee to Green-land for a haunch of venison, just of the thickness of thine own tallow.

CLOWN
Ha, ha, ha, I'll not stir an inch for thee.

FOROBOSCO
Thence to Amboyna i'th' East-Indies, for pepper to bake it.

CLOWN
To Amboyna? so I might be pepper'd.

FOROBOSCO
Then will I conveigh thee stark naked to Develing to beg a pair of brogs, to hide thy mountainous buttocks.

CLOWN
And no doublet to 'em?

FOROBOSCO
No sir, I intend to send you of a sleeveless errand; but before you vanish, in regard you say I cannot conjure, and are so stupid, and opinionated a slave, that neither I, nor my art can compell you to do any thing that's beyond your own pleasure, the gentlemen shall have some sport, you cannot endure a cat sirra?

CLOWN
What's that to thee Jugler?

FOROBOSCO
Nor you'll do nothing at my entreaty?

CLOWN
I'll be hang'd first.

FOROBOSCO
Sit Gentlemen, and whatsoever you see, be not frighted.

HOSTESS
Alas I can endure no conjuring.

HOST
Stir not wife.

BIANCA
Pray let me go sir, I am not fit for these fooleryes.

HOST
Move not daughter.

FOROBOSCO
I wil make you dance a new dance call'd leap-frog.

CLOWN
Ha, ha, ha.

FOROBOSCO
And as naked as a frog.

CLOWN

Ha, ha, ha, I defie thee.

[**FOROBOSCO** looks in a book, strikes with his wand, Musick playes.

[Enter **FOUR BOYS** shaped like Frogs, and dance.

PEDANT
Spirits of the water in the likeness of frogs.

TAILOR
He has fisht fair believe me.

MULETIER
See, see, he sweats and trembles.

FOROBOSCO
Are you come to your quavers?

CLOWN
Oh, ho, ho.

FOROBOSCO
I'll make you run division on that o'r ere I leave you; looke you, here are the playfellowes that are so indear'd to you; come sir, first uncase, and then dance, nay I'll make him dance stark naked.

HOST
Oh let him have his shirt on and his Mogols breeches, here are Women ith' house.

FOROBOSCO
Well for their sakes he shall.

[**CLOWN** teares off his doublet, making strange faces as if compel'd to it, falls into the Dance.

TAILOR
He dances, what a lying rogue was this to say the gentleman could not conjure!

FOROBOSCO
He does prettily well, but 'tis voluntary, I assure you, I have no hand in't.

CLOWN
As you are a Counjurer, and a rare Artist, free me from these couplets; of all creatures I cannot endure a Frog.

FOROBOSCO
But your dancing is voluntary, I can compell you to nothing.

HOSTESS
O me, daughter, lets take heed of this fellow, he'll make us dance naked, an' we vex him.

[Exeunt **HOSTESS** and **BIANCA**.

FOROBOSCO
Now cut capers sirra, I'll plague that chine of yours.

CLOWN
Ho, ho, ho, my kidneys are rosted. I drop away like a pound of butter rosted.

TAILOR
He will dance himself to death.

FOROBOSCO
No matter I'll sell his fat to the Pothecaries, and repair my injury that way.

HOST
Enough in conscience.

FOROBOSCO
Well, at your entreaty vanish. And now I wil only make him break his neck in doing a sommerset, and that's all the revenge I mean to take of him.

CLOWN
O gentlemen, what a rogue was I to belye so an approved Master in the noble dark science? you can witness, this I did only to spoyle his practise and deprive you of the happyness of injoying his worthy labors; rogue that I was to do it, pray sir forgive me.

FOROBOSCO
With what face canst thou ask it?

CLOWN
With such a face as I deserve, with a hanging look, as all here can testifie.

FOROBOSCO
Well gentlemen, that you may perceive the goodness of my temper, I will entertain this rogue againe in hope of amendment, for should I turn him off, he would be hang'd.

CLOWN
You may read that in this foul coppy.

FOROBOSCO
Only with this promise, you shall never cozen any of my patients.

CLOWN
Never.

FOROBOSCO

And remember hence forward, that though I cannot conjure, I can make you dance sirra, go get your self into the cottage again.

[Enter **CESARIO**.

CLOWN
I will never more dance leap-Frog: now I have got you into credit, hold it up, and cozen them in abundance.

FOROBOSCO
Oh rare rascall.

[Exit **CLOWN**.

CESARIO
How now, a Frankford mart here, a Mountebank, and his worshipfull auditory?

HOST
They are my guests Sir.

CESARIO
A pox upon them, shew your jugling tricks in some other room.

HOST
And why not here Sir?

CESARIO
Hence, or sirra I shall spoil your figure flinging, and all their radicall questions.

OMNES
Sir we vanish.

[Exeunt. Manet **HOST** & **CESARIO**.

HOST
Signior Cesario, you make bold with me,
And somewhat I must tell you to a degree
Of ill manners: they are my guests, and men I live by,
And I would know by what authority
You command thus far.

CESARIO
By my interest in your daughter.

HOST
Interest do you call't? as I remember I never put her out to Usury on that condition.

CESARIO

Pray thee be not angry.

[Enter **BIANCA** and **HOSTESS**.

I am come to make thee happy, and her happy:
She's here; alas my pretty soul, I am come
To give assurance that's beyond thy hope,
Or thy beleif, I bring repentance 'bout me,
And satisfaction, I will marry thee.

BIANCA
Ha?

CESARIO
As I live I will, but do not entertain't
With too quick an apprehension of joy,
For that may hurt thee, I have heard some dye of't.

BIANCA
Do not fear me.

CESARIO
Then thou think'st I feign
This protestation, I will instantly
Before these testifie my new alliance,
Contract my self unto thee, then I hope
We may be more private.

HOST
But thou shalt not sir,
For so has many a maiden-head been lost, and many a bastard gotten.

CESARIO
Then to give you the best of any assurance in the world,
Entreat thy father to go fetch a Preist
Wee will instantly to bed, and there be married.

BIANCA
Pride hath not yet forsaken you I see,
Though prosperity has.

HOST
Sir you are too confident
To fashion to your self a dream of purchase
When you are a begger.

CESARIO
You are bold with me.

HOSTESS
Doe we not know your value is cried down
Fourscore i'th' hundred.

BIANCA
Oh sir I did love you
With such a fixed heart, that in that minute
Wherein you slighted, or contemn'd me rather,
I took a vow to obey your last decree,
And never more look up at any hope
Should bring me comfort that way: and though since
Your Foster-mother, and the fair Clarissa
Have in the way of marriage despis'd you,
That hath not any way bred my revenge,
But compassion rather. I have found
So much sorrow in the way to a chaste wedlock
That here I will set down, and never wish
To come to'th' journies end. Your suit to mee
Henceforth be ever silenc'd.

CESARIO
My Bianca.

HOSTESS
Henceforward pray forbear her and my house:
She's a poor virtuous wench, yet her estate
May weigh with yours in a gold balance.

HOST
Yes, and her birth in any Heralds office in
Christendom.

HOSTESS
It may prove so:
When you'll say, you have leapt a Whiting.

[Exit.

[Enter **BAPTISTA** and **MENTIVOLE**.

CESARIO
How far am I grown behind hand with fortune!

BAPTISTA
Here's Cesario!
My son Sir, is to morrow to be married
Unto the fair Clarissa.

CESARIO
So.

MENTIVOLE
Wee hope you'll be a guest there.

CESARIO
No I will not grace your triumph so much.

BAPTISTA
I will not tax your breeding.
But it alters not your birth Sir, fare you well.

MENTIVOLE
Oh Sir, doe not greive him,
He has too much affliction already.

[Exeunt.

[Enter a **SAILOR**.

CESARIO
Every way scorn'd and lost,
Shame follow you
For I am grown most miserable.

SAILOR
Sir do you know a Ladies son in town here
They cal Cesario?

CESARIO
There's none such I assure thee.

SAILOR
I was told you were the man.

CESARIO
What's that to thee?

SAILOR
A — on't. You are melancholy, will you drink Sir?

CESARIO
With whom?

SAILOR

With me Sir; despise not this pitch'd Canvas; the time was we have known them lin'd with Spanish
Duckets; I have news for you:

CESARIO
For me!

SAILOR
Not unless you'll drink;
We are like our Sea provision, once out of pickle,
We require abundance of drink; I have news to tell you,
That were you Prince,
Would make you send your mandate
To have a thousand bonfires made i'th' City
And pist out agen with nothing but Greek wine.

CESARIO
Come, I will drink with thee howsoever.

SAILOR
And upon these terms I will utter my mind to you.

[Exeunt.

SCÆNA PRIMA

Enter **ALBERTO, PROSPERO, JULIANA** and **SAILORS**.

SAILOR
Shall we bring your necessaries ashore my Lord?

ALBERTO
Do what you please, I am land-sick, worse by far
Than ere I was at sea.

PROSPERO
Collect your self.

ALBERTO
O my most worthy Prospero, my best friend,
The noble favor I receiv'd from thee
In freeing me from the Turks I now accompt
Worse than my death; for I shall never live
To make requitall; what do you attend for?

SAILORS
To understand your pleasure.

ALBERTO
They do mock me;
I do protest I have no kind of pleasure
In any thing i'th' world, but in thy friendship,
I must ever except that.

PROSPERO
Pray leave him, leave him.—

[Exeunt **SAILORS**.

ALBERTO
The news I heard related since my landing
Of the division of my Family,
How is it possible for any man
To bear't with a set patience?

PROSPERO
You have suffer'd
Since your imprisonment more waighty sorrows.

ALBERTO
I, then I was man of flesh and blood,
Now I am made up of fire, to the full height
Of a deadly Calenture; O these vild women
That are so ill preservers of mens honors,
They cannot govern their own honesties.
That I should thirty and odd winters feed
My expectation of a noble heir,
And by a womans falshood find him now
A fiction, a mere dream of what he was;
And yet I love him still.

PROSPERO
In my opinion
The sentence (on this tryall) from the Duke
Was noble, to repair Cesario's loss
With the marriage of your wife, had you been dead.

ALBERTO
By your favor but it was not, I conceive
T' was disparagement to my name, to have my widdow
Match with a Faulkeiners son, and yet beli've't
I love the youth still, and much pitty him.
I do remember at my going to Sea,

Upon a quarrel, and a hurt receiv'd
From young Mentivole, my rage so far
Oretopt my nobler temper, I gave charge
To have his hand cut off, which since I heard,
And to my comfort, brave Cesario,
Worthyly prevented.

PROSPERO
And 'twas nobly done.

ALBERTO
Yet the revenge, for this intent of mine
Hath bred much slaughter in our families,
And yet my wife (which infinitely moans me)
Intends to marry my sole heir Clarissa
To the head branch of the other faction.

PROSPERO
'Tis the mean to work reconcilement.

ALBERTO
Between whom?

PROSPERO
Your self and the worthy Baptista.

ALBERTO
Never.

PROSPERO
O you have been of a noble and remarkable friendship,
And by this match 'tis generally in Florence
Hop'd, 'twill fully be reconcil'd; to me
'Twould be absolute content.

JULIANA
And to my self, I have main interest in it.

ALBERTO
Noble Sir, you may command my heart to break for you
But never to bend that way; poor Cesario,
When thou put'st on thy mournfull willow-garland,
Thy enemy shall be suted (I do vow)
In the same livery, my Cesario
Loved as my foster child, though not my Son,
Which in some countryes formerly were barbarous,
Was a name held most affectionate; thou art lost,
Unfortunate young man, not only slighted

Where thou received'st thy breeding, but since scorn'd
I th' way of marriage, by the poor Bianca
The In-keepers daughter.

PROSPERO
I have heard of that too;
But let not that afflict you: for this Lady
May happily deliver at more leasure
A circumstance may draw a fair event,
Better than you can hope for.
For this present we must leave you,
And shall visit you again within these two hours.

[Enter **CESARIO**.

ALBERTO
Ever to me most welcome,—O my Cesario.

CESARIO
I am none of yours Sir, so 'tis protested;
And I humbly beg,
Since 'tis not in your power to preserve me
Any longer in a noble course of life,
Give me a worthy death.

ALBERTO
The youth is mad.

CESARIO
Nay Sir, I will instruct you in a way
To kill me honorably.

ALBERTO
That were most strange.

CESARIO
I am turning Pirate, You may be imployed
By the Duke to fetch me in; and in a Sea-fight
Give me a noble grave.

ALBERTO
Questionless he's mad: I would give any Doctor
A thousand crowns to free him from this sorrow.

CESARIO
Here's the Physitian.—

[Shewes a Poniard.

ALBERTO
Hold Sir, I did say
To free you from the sorrow, not from life.

CESARIO
Why life and sorrow are unseparable.

ALBERTO
Be comforted Cesario, Mentivole
Shall not marry Clarissa.

CESARIO
No Sir, ere he shall, I'll kill him.

ALBERTO
But you forfeit your own life then.

CESARIO
That's worth nothing.

ALBERTO
Cesario, be thy self, be mine Cesario:
Make not thy self uncapable of that portion
I have full purpose to confer upon thee,
By falling into madness: bear thy wrongs
With noble patience, the afflicted's friend
Which ever in all actions crowns the end.

CESARIO
You well awak'd me; nay recover'd me
Both to sence and full life, O most noble sir,
Though I have lost my fortune, and lost you
For a worthy Father: yet I will not lose
My former virtue, my integrity
Shall not yet forsake me; but as the wild Ivy,
Spreads and thrives better in some pittious ruin
Of tower, or defac'd Temple, than it does
Planted by a new building; so shall I
Make my adversity my instrument
To winde me up into a full content.

ALBERTO
'Tis worthily resolv'd; our first adventure
Is to stop the marriage; for thy other losses,
Practis'd by a womans malice, but account them
Like conjurers winds rais'd to a fearfull blast,
And do some mischeif, but do never last.

[Exeunt.

[Enter **FOROBOSCO** and **CLOWN**.

CLOWN
Now sir, will you not acknowledge that I have mightily advanc'd your practice?

FOROBOSCO
'Tis confest, and I will make thee a great man for't.

CLOWN
I take a course to do that my self, for I drink sack in abundance.

FOROBOSCO
O my rare rascall! We must remove.

CLOWN
Whither?

FOROBOSCO
Any whither: Europe is too little to be coz'ned by us, I am ambitious to go to the East-Indies, thou and I to ride on our brace of Elephants.

CLOWN
And for my part I long to be in England agen; you will never get so much as in England, we have shifted many countryes, and many names: but trance the world over you shall never purse up so much gold as when you were in England, and call'd your self Doctor Lambe-stones.

FOROBOSCO
'Twas an atractive name I confess, women were then my only admirers.

CLOWN
And all their visits was either to further their lust, or revenge injuries.

FOROBOSCO
You should have forty in a morning beleaguer my closet, and strive who should be cozen'd first, amongst four-score love-sick waiting women that has come to me in a morning to learn what fortune should betide them in their first marriage, I have found above 94 to have lost their maiden-heads.

CLOWN
By their own confession, but I was fain to be your male midwife, and work it out of them by circumstance.

FOROBOSCO
Thou wast, and yet for all this frequent resort of women and thy handling of their urinals and their cases, thou art not given to lechery, what should be the reason of it? Thou hast wholsome flesh enough about thee; me thinks the divell should tempt thee to't.

CLOWN

What need he do that, when he makes me his instrument to tempt others.

FOROBOSCO

Thou canst not chuse but utter thy rare good parts; thou wast an excellent baud I acknowledge.

CLOWN

Well, and what I have done that way, I will spare to speak of all you and I have done sir, and though we should—

FOROBOSCO

We will for England, that's for certain.

CLOWN

We shall never want there.

FOROBOSCO

Want? their Court of Wards shall want money first: for I profess my self Lord Paramount over fools and madfolkes.

CLOWN

Do but store your self with lyes enough against you come thither.

FOROBOSCO

Why that's all the familiarity I ever had with the Divell, my guift of lying, they say he's the Father of lyes; and though I cannot conjure, yet I profess my self to be one of his poor gossips. I will now reveale to thee a rare peece of service.

CLOWN

What is it my most worshipful Doctor Lamb-stones?

FOROBOSCO

There is a Captain come lately from Sea,
They call Prosper, I saw him this morning
Through a chink of wainscote that divides my lodging,

And the Host of the house, withdraw my Host, and Hostess, the fair Bianca, and an antient gentlewoman into their bedchamber; I could not overhear their conference, but I saw such a mass of gold & Jewels, & when he had done he lock't it up into a casket; great joy there was amongst them, & forth they are gone into the city, and my Host told me at his going forth he thought he should not return till after supper: now Sir, in their absence will we fall to our picklocks, enter the chamber, seize the Jewels, make an escape from Florence, and we are made for ever.

CLOWN

But if they should go to a true conjurer, and fetch us back in a whirle-wind?

FOROBOSCO

Do not believe there is any such fetch in Astrology, and this may be a means to make us live honest hereafter.

CLOWN
'Tis but an ill road to't that lyes through the high way of theeving.

FOROBOSCO
For indeed I am weary of this trade of fortune-telling; and mean to give all over, when I come into England, for it is a very ticklish quality.

CLOWN
And i'th' end will hang by a twine thred.

FOROBOSCO
Besides the Island has too many of the profession, they hinder one anothers market.

CLOWN
No, no, the pillory hinders their market.

FOROBOSCO
You know there the jugling captain.

CLOWN
I there's a sure card.

FOROBOSCO
Only the fore-man of their jury is dead, but he dyed like a Roman.

CLOWN
Else 'tis thought he had made work for the hangman.

FOROBOSCO
And the very Ball, of your false prophets, he's quasht too.

CLOWN
He did measure the stars with a false yard, and may now travail to Rome, with a morter on's head to see if he can recover his money that way.

FOROBOSCO
Come, come, lets fish for this casket, and to Sea presently.

CLOWN
We shall never reach London, I fear;
My mind runs so much of hanging, landing at Wapping.

[Exeunt.

[Enter **MARIANA**.

This well may be a day of joy long wish'd for
To my Clarissa, she is innocent.
Nor can her youth but with an open bosome
Meet Hymens pleasing bounties, but to me
That am inviron'd with black guilt and horror
It does appear a funeral though promising much
In the conception were hard to mannage
But sad in the event, it was not hate
But fond indulgence in me to preserve
Cesario's threatn'd life in open court
Then forc'd me to disclaime him, choosing rather
To rob him of his birthright, and honor
Than suffer him to run the hazard of
Inrag'd Baptista's fury, while he lives;
I know I have a Son, and the Dukes sentence
A while deluded, and this tempest over,
When he assures himself despair hath seiz'd him.

[Knock within.

[Enter **BAPTISTA**.

I can relieve and raise him—speak, who is it
That presses on my privacies? Sir your pardon.
You cannot come unwelcome, though it were
To read my secret thoughts.

BAPTISTA
Lady to you
Mine shall be ever open; Lady said I,
That name keeps too much distance, sister rather
I should have stil'd you, and I now may claime it,
Since our divided families are made one
By this blessed marriage; to whose honor comes
The Duke in person, waited on by all
The braveries of his Court, to witness it,
And then to be our ghests, is the bride ready
To meet and entertain him?

MARIANA
She attends the comming of your Son.

BAPTISTA
Pray you bring her forth.
The Duke's at hand—Musick, in her loud voyce,
Speaks his arrivall.

MARIANA
She's prepar'd to meet it.

[Exit.

[Enter **MARIANA**, **CLARISSA**, led by **TWO MAIDS**: at the other door, **BAPTISTA** meets with **MENTIVOLE**, led by **TWO COURTIERS**, the **DUKE of FLORENCE**, **BISHOP**; **DIVERS**, **ATTENDANTS**: A Song, whilst they salute.

DUKE of FLORENCE
It were impertinent to wish you joy,
Since all joyes dwell about you, Hymens torch
Was never lighted with a luckier Omen.
Nor burnt with so much splendor, to defer
With fruitless compliment, the means to make
Your certain pleasures lawful to the world;
Since in the union of your hearts they are
Confirm'd already: would but argue us
A boaster of our favours; to the Temple,
And there the sacred knot once ti'd, all triumphs
Our Dukedom can afford, shall grace your Nuptials.

[Enter **ALBERTO** and **CESARIO**.

BAPTISTA
On there.

MENTIVOLE
I hope it is not in the power
Of any to cross us now.

ALBERTO
But in the breath
Of a wrong'd Father I forbid the Banes.

CESARIO
What, do you stand at gaze?

BAPTISTA
Risen from the dead!

MARIANA
Although the Sea had vomited up the Figure
In which thy better part liv'd long imprison'd,
True love despising fear, runs thus to meet it.

CLARISSA
In duty I kneel to it.

ALBERTO

Hence vile wretches,
To you I am a substance incorporeal,
And not to be prophan'd, with your vile touch?
That could so soon forget me, but such things
Are neither worth my Anger, nor reproof.
To you great Sir, I turn my self and these
Immediate Ministers of your Government,
And if in my rude language I transgress;
Ascribe it to the cold remembrance of
My services, and not my rugged temper.

DUKE of FLORENCE

Speak freely, be thy language ne'er so bitter,
To see thee safe Alberto, signes thy pardon.

ALBERTO

My pardon? I can need none, if it be not
Receiv'd for an offence. I tamely bear
Wrongs, which a slave-born Muscovite would check at.
Why if for Treason I had been deliver'd
Up to the Hangmans Axe, and this dead trunk
Unworthy of a Christian Sepulchre;
Expos'd a prey to feed the ravenous Vulture,
The memory of the much I oft did for you,
Had you but any touch of gratitude,
Or thought of my deservings, would have stopp'd you
From these unjust proceedings.

DUKE of FLORENCE

Hear the motives that did induce us.

ALBERTO

I have heard them all,
Your Highness sentence, the whole Court abus'd,
By the perjuries and practice of this woman.
(Wepest thou Crocodile) my hopeful son,
Whom I dare swear mine own, degraded of
The honors that descend to him from me:
And from that, in his love scorn'd by a creature
Whose base birth, though made eminent by her beauty,
Might well have mark'd her out Cesario's servant,
All this I could have pardon'd and forgot;
But that my daughter with my whole Estate
So hardly purchas'd, is assign'd a Dower;
To one whose Father, and whose Family
I so detest; that I would lose my essence

And be transformed to a Basiliske
To look them dead, to me's an injury
Admits no satisfaction.

BAPTISTA
There's none offer'd.

ALBERTO
Nor would not be accepted,
Though upon thy knees 'twere tender'd.

MARIANA
Now the storm grows high.

BAPTISTA
But that I thought thee dead, and in thy death
The brinie Ocean had entomb'd thy name;
I would have sought a Wife in a Bordello
For my Mentivole, and gladly hugg'd
Her spurious issue as my lawful Nephews,
Before his blood should e'er have mix'd with thine;
So much I scorn it.

ALBERTO
I'll not bandy words, but thus dissolve the contract.

BAPTISTA
There I meet thee, and seize on what's mine own.

ALBERTO
For all my service,
Great Sir, grant me the combat with this wretch,
That I may scourge his insolence.

BAPTISTA
I kneel for it.

CESARIO
And to approve my self Alberto's Son,
I'll be his second upon any odds,
'Gainst him that dare most of Baptista's race.

MENTIVOLE
Already upon honourable terms,
In me thou hast met thy better, for her sake
I'll add no more.

ALBERTO

Sir, let our swords decide it.

MARIANA
Oh stay Sir, and as you would hold the Title
Of a just Prince, e'r you grant licence to
These mad-mens fury, lend your private ear
To the most distress'd of Women.

DUKE of FLORENCE
Speak, 'tis granted.

[He takes **MARIANA** aside.

CLARISSA
In the mean time, let not Clarissa be
A patient looker on, though as yet doubtful,
To whom to bend her knee first, yet to all
I stoop thus low in duty, and would wash
The dust of fury with my Virgin tears,
From his bless'd feet, and make them beautiful
That would move to conditions of peace,
Though with a snail-like pace, they all are wing'd
To bear you to destruction: reverend Sirs,
Think on your antient friendship cemented
With so much bloud, but shed in noble action,
Divided now in passion for a brawl;
The Makers blush to own, much lov'd Cesario.
Brother, or friend, (each Title may prevail,)
Remember with what tenderness from our childhood
We lov'd together, you preferring me
Before your self, and I so fond of you
That it begot suspition in ill minds
That our affection was incestuous.
Think of that happy time, in which I know
That with your dearest bloud you had prevented
This shower of tears from me; Mentivole,
My Husband, registred in that bright star-chamber,
Though now on earth made strangers, be the example
And offer in one hand the peaceful Olive
Of concord, or if that can be denied
By powerful intercession in the other
Carry the Hermian rod, and force attonement,
Now we will not be all marble. Death's the worst then
And he shall be my Bridegroom.

[Offers to kill her self.

MENTIVOLE

Hold Clarissa, his loving violence needs must
Offer in spite of honor.—

[He snatches away her knife, and sets it to his own breast, she staies his hand.

DUKE of FLORENCE
Was it to that end then on your Religion?

MARIANA
And my hope in Heaven, Sir.

DUKE of FLORENCE
We then will leave intreaties, and make use
Of our authority, must I cry ai-me
To this unheard of insolence? in my presence
To draw your swords, and as all reverence
That's due to Majesty were forfeited,
Cherish this wildeness! sheath them instantly,
And shew an alteration in your looks, or by my power.

ALBERTO
Cut off my head.

BAPTISTA
And mine, rather than hear of peace with this bad man.
I'll not alone, give up my throat, but suffer
Your rage to reach my family.

[Enter **PROSPERO, JLIANA, BIANCA.**

ALBERTO
And my name to be no more remembred.

DUKE of FLORENCE
What are these?

CESARIO
Bianca, 'tis Bianca, still Bianca: but strangely alter'd.

BAPTISTA
If that thirteen years
Of absence could raze from my memory
The figure of my friend, I might forget thee;
But if thy Image be graven on my heart,
Thou art my Prospero.

PROSPERO
Thou my Baptista?

DUKE of FLORENCE
A suddain change!

BAPTISTA
I dare not ask, dear friend
If Juliana live! for that's a blessing
I am unworthy of, but yet denie not
To let me know the place she hath made happy
By having there her Sepulchre.

PROSPERO
If your Highness please to vouchsafe a patient
Ear, we shall make a true relation of a story
That shall call on your wonder.

DUKE of FLORENCE
Speak, we hear you.

PROSPERO
Baptista's fortune in the Genoua Court,
His banishment, with his fair Wife's restraint
You are acquainted with; what since hath follow'd
I faithfully will deliver. E'r eight Moons
After Baptista's absence were compleat,
Fair Juliana found the pleasures, that
They had injoy'd together, were not barren,
And blushing at the burthen of her womb,
No father near to own it, it drew on
A violent sickness, which call'd down compassion
From the angry Duke, then careful of her health.
Physitians were enquir'd of, and their judgment
Prescrib'd the Baths of Luca as a means
For her recovery; to my charge it pleas'd her
To be committed; but as on the way
We journey'd, those throws only known to Women
Came thick upon her, in a private Village.

BAPTISTA
She died?

PROSPERO
Have patience, she brought to the world
A hopeful Daughter; for her bodies sickness
It soon decay'd, but the grief of her mind
Hourly increas'd, and life grew tedious to her,
And desperate e'er to see you; she injoyn'd me
To place her in a Greekish Monastery,

And to my care gave up her pretty Daughter.

BAPTISTA
What Monastery? as a Pilgrim bare-foot,
I'll search it out.

PROSPERO
Pray you interrupt me not,
Now to my fortunes; the girl well dispos'd of
With a faithful friend of mine, my cruel fate
Made me a prisoner to the Turkish Gallies,
Where for 12 years, these hands tugg'd at the Oar,
But fortune tyr'd at length with my afflictions,
Some Ships of Maltha met the Ottoman Fleet,
Charg'd them, and boarded them, and gave me freedom.
With my deliverers I serv'd, and got
Such reputation with the great Master
That he gave me command over a tall
And lusty ship, where my first happy service
Was to redeem Alberto rumour'd dead,
But was like me surpriz'd by Cortugogly.

ALBERTO
I would I had died there.

PROSPERO
And from him learning
Baptista liv'd, and their dissolv'd friendship,
I hois'd up sails for Greece, found Juliana
A votary at her Beads; having made known
Both that you liv'd, and where you were: she borrow'd
So much from her devotion, as to wish me
To bring her to you; if the object please you,
With joy receive her.

BAPTISTA
Rage and fury leave me.

[Throws away his sword.

I am so full of happiness, there's no room left
To entertain you, oh my long lost Jewel,
Light of mine eyes, my souls strength.

JULIANA
My best Lord, having embrac'd you thus,
Death cannot fright me.

BAPTISTA
Live long to do so, though I should fix here.
Pardon me Prospero, though I enquire my daughters fortune.

PROSPERO
That your happiness
May be at all parts perfect, here she is!

CESARIO
Bianca, daughter to a Princess.

PROSPERO
True with my faithful Host I left her,
And with him till now she hath resided,
Ignorant both of her birth and greatness.

BAPTISTA
Oh my blest one. Joy upon joy o'erwhelms me.

DUKE of FLORENCE
Above wonder.

ALBERTO
I do begin to melt too, this strange story
Works much upon me.

DUKE of FLORENCE
Since it hath pleas'd heaven
To grace us with this miracle, I that am
Heavens instrument here, determine thus; Alberto
Be not unthankful for the blessings shown you,
Nor you Baptista; discord was yet never
A welcome sacrifice; therefore rage laid by,
Embrace as friends, and let pass'd difference
Be as a dream forgotten.

BAPTISTA
'Tis to me.

ALBERTO
And me, and thus confirm it.

DUKE of FLORENCE
And to tye it
In bonds not to be broken, with the marriage
Of young Mentivole, and fair Clarissa,
So you consent great Lady, your Bianca
Shall call Cæsario Husband.

JULIANA
'Tis a motion I gladly yield to.

CESARIO
One in which you make a sad man happy.

[Offers to kneel.

BIANCA
Kneel not, all forgiven.

DUKE of FLORENCE
With the Duke your Uncle I will make attonement, and will have no denial.

[Enter **HOST**, **FOROBOSCO**, **CLOWN** and **OFFICERS**.

MARIANA
Let this day be still held sacred.

HOST
Now if you can conjure, let the Devil unbind you.

FOROBOSCO
We are both undone.

CLOWN
Already we feel it.

HOST
Justice Sir.

DUKE of FLORENCE
What are they?

PROSPERO
I can resolve you, slaves freed from the Gallies
By the Viceroy of Sicilia.

DUKE of FLORENCE
What's their offence?

HOST
The robbing me of all my Plate and Jewels, I mean the attempting of it.

CLOWN

Please your Grace I will now discover this Varlet in earnest, this honest pestilent rogue, profest the Art of Conjuring, but all the skill that ever he had in the black Art, was in making a Seacole fire; only with wearing strange shapes, he begot admiration amongst Fools and Women.

FOROBOSCO
Wilt thou peach thou varlet?

DUKE of FLORENCE
Why does he goggle with his eyes, and stalke so?

CLOWN
This is one of his Magical raptures.

FOROBOSCO
I do vilifie your censure, you demand if I am guilty, whir says my cloak by a trick of Legerdemain, now I am not guilty, I am guarded with innocence, pure Silver Lace I assure you.

CLOWN
Thus have I read to you your virtues, which notwithstanding I would not have you proud of.

FOROBOSCO
Out thou concealment of Tallow, and counterfeit Mummia.

DUKE of FLORENCE
To the Gallies with them both.

CLOWN
The only Sea-physick for a knave, is to be basted in a
Gally, with the oil of a Bulls Peesel.

FOROBOSCO
And will not you make a sour face at the same sauce, sirrah? I hope to find thee so lean in one fortnight, thou mayst be drawn by the ears through the hoop of a firkin.

DUKE of FLORENCE
Divide them, and away with them to th' Gallies.

CLOWN
This will take down your pride, Jugler.

DUKE of FLORENCE
This day that hath given birth to blessings beyond hope, admits no criminal sentence: to the Temple, and there with humbleness, praise heavens bounties;
For blessings ne'er descend from thence, but when
A sacrifice in thanks ascends from men.

[Exeunt **OMNES**.

John Fletcher – A Short Biography

John Fletcher was born in December, 1579 in Rye, Sussex. He was baptised on December 20th.

As can be imagined details of much of his life and career have not survived and, accordingly, only a very brief indication of his life and works can be given.

His father, Richard Fletcher, was a successful and rather ambitious cleric. From being the Dean of Peterborough he moved on to become the Bishop of Bristol, Bishop of Worcester and finally, shortly before his death, the Bishop of London. He was also the chaplain to Queen Elizabeth.

When he was Dean of Peterborough, Richard Fletcher, witnessed the execution of Mary, Queen of Scots. It was said he "knelt down on the scaffold steps and started to pray out loud and at length, in a prolonged and rhetorical style, as though determined to force his way into the pages of history". He cried out at her death, "So perish all the Queen's enemies!" All very dramatic but the family did have strong links to the Arts.

Young Fletcher appears at the very young age of eleven to have entered Corpus Christi College at Cambridge University in 1591. There are no records that he ever took a degree but there is some small evidence that he was being prepared for a career in the church.

However what is clear is that this was soon abandoned as he joined the stream of people who would leave University and decamp to the more bohemian life of commercial theatre in London.

Unfortunately his father fell out with Queen Elizabeth but appears to have been on his way to rehabilitation before his death in 1596. At his death he was, however, mired in debt.

The upbringing of the now teenage Fletcher and his seven siblings now passed to his paternal uncle, the poet and minor official Giles Fletcher. Giles, who had the patronage of the Earl of Essex may have been a liability rather than an advantage to the young Fletcher. With Essex involved in the failed rebellion against Elizabeth Giles was also tainted by association.

By 1606 John Fletcher appears to have equipped himself with the talents to become a playwright. Initially this appears to have been for the Children of the Queen's Revels, then performing at the Blackfriars Theatre.

Commendatory verses by Richard Brome in the Beaumont and Fletcher 1647 folio place Fletcher in the company of Ben Jonson, although it is not known when this friendship began. Jonson, of course, was a leviathan of English Literature, so admired that many of his literary friends and colleagues were simply known as 'Sons of Ben'. Fletcher's frequent early collaborator, Francis Beaumont, was also a friend of Jonson's.

Fletcher's early career was marked by one significant failure; The Faithful Shepherdess, his adaptation of Giovanni Battista Guarini's Il Pastor Fido, which was performed by the Blackfriars Children in 1608. In the preface to the printed edition of his play, Fletcher explained the failure as due to his audience's faulty expectations. They expected a pastoral tragicomedy to feature dances, comedy, and murder, with the shepherds presented in conventional stereotypes – as Fletcher put it, wearing "gray cloaks, with curtailed dogs in strings." Fletcher's preface is however best known for its pithy definition of tragicomedy: "A tragicomedy is not so called in respect of mirth and killing, but in respect it wants [i.e., lacks] deaths, which is enough to make it no tragedy; yet brings some near it, which is enough to make it no comedy." A comedy, he went on to say, must be "a representation of familiar people." His preface is critical of drama that features characters whose action violates nature.

In that case, Fletcher appears to have been developing a new style faster than audiences could comprehend. By 1609, however, he had found his stride. With Beaumont, he wrote Philaster, which became a hit for the King's Men and began a profitable association between Fletcher and that company. Philaster appears also to have begun a trend for tragicomedy. Fletcher's influence has also been said to have inspired some features of Shakespeare's late romances, and certainly his influence on the tragicomic work of other playwrights is even more marked.

By the middle of the 1610s, Fletcher's plays had achieved a popularity that rivalled Shakespeare's and cemented the pre-eminence of the King's Men in Jacobean London. After Beaumont's retirement, necessitated by ill-health, and then his early death in 1616, Fletcher continued working, both singly and in collaboration, until his death in 1625. By that time, he had produced, or had been credited with, close to fifty plays. This body of work remained a major part of the King's Men's repertory until the closing of the theatres in 1642 due to the Civil War.

At the beginning of his career Fletcher's most important collaborator was Francis Beaumont. The two wrote together for close to a decade, first for the Children of the Queen's Revels, and then for the King's Men. According to an anecdote transmitted or invented by John Aubrey, they also lived together in Bankside, sharing clothes and having "one wench in the house between them." This domestic arrangement, if it existed, was ended by Beaumont's marriage in 1613, and their dramatic partnership ended after Beaumont fell ill, probably of a stroke, that same year.

At this point Fletcher had written many plays with Beaumont and several others on his own. He seems to have been regarded as quite a talent although it should be remembered that playwrights were required to be prolific, to easily work with other collaborators and to produce work of quality and commercial appeal very quickly.

The King's Men, run by Philip Henslowe, was the most prestigious of the theatre companies and Fletcher now had an increasingly close association with it.

Fletcher collaborated with Shakespeare on Henry VIII, The Two Noble Kinsmen, and the now lost Cardenio, which some scholars say was the basis for Lewis Theobald's play Double Falsehood. (Theobald is regarded as one of the best Shakespearean editors. Whether his play is based on Cardenio or on some other is not absolutely known although Theobald certainly promoted it as his revision of the lost Shakespeare/Fletcher play.)

A play that Fletcher also wrote by himself at this time, The Woman's Prize or the Tamer Tamed, is also regarded as a sequel to The Taming of the Shrew.

In 1616, with the death of Shakespeare, Fletcher now appears to have entered into an enhanced arrangement with the King's Men on very similar terms to Shakespeare's. Fletcher would now write exclusively for the King's Men until his own death almost a decade later.

As well as continuing his solo productions Fletcher was still collaborating with other playwrights, mainly Philip Massinger, who, in turn, would succeed him as the in-house playwright for the King's Men.

Fletcher's popularity continued throughout his life; indeed during the winter of 1621, he had three of his plays performed at court. His mastery is most notable in two dramatic types; tragicomedy and the comedy of manners.

John Fletcher died in 1625, it is thought of bubonic plague which, at the time, was undergoing further outbreaks.

He seems to have been buried in what is now Southwark Cathedral, although a precise location is not known. There is much made of an anecdote that Fletcher and Massinger (who died in 1640) share the same grave but it is more likely that both are buried within a few yards of each other and that the stone markers in the floor have confused the issue. One is marked 'Edmond Shakespeare 1607' and the other 'John Fletcher 1625' refers to Shakespeare's younger brother and the playwright. The churchyards were, more often than not, completely over-crowded and breeding grounds for disease. Precise record keeping was not a practiced skill.

During the later Commonwealth, many of the playwright's best-known scenes were kept alive as drolls. These were brief performances, usually condensed into one or two scenes and with the addition of music or song to satisfy the taste for plays while the theatres were closed under the Puritans. At the re-opening of the theatres in 1660, the plays in the Fletcher canon, in original form or revised, were by far the most common productions on the English stage. The most frequently revived plays suggest the developing taste for comedies of manners. Among the tragedies, The Maid's Tragedy and, especially, Rollo Duke of Normandy held the stage. Four tragicomedies (A King and No King, The Humorous Lieutenant, Philaster, and The Island Princess) were popular, perhaps in part for their similarity to and foreshadowing of heroic drama. Four comedies (Rule a Wife And Have a Wife, The Chances, Beggars' Bush, and especially The Scornful Lady) were also stage mainstays.

Despite his popularity, and it appears he was held in higher regard than Shakespeare at this time, his works steadily lost ground to those of Shakespeare and to new productions from other playwrights.

Since then Fletcher has increasingly become a subject only for occasional revivals and for specialists. Fletcher and his collaborators have been the subject of important bibliographic and critical studies, but the plays have been revived only infrequently.

Due to the frequent collaborations between all manner of playwrights, and the revisions carried out in later years, having a settled list of authorship to any given set of plays can be problematic. The works of Fletcher and others of this period most definitely fall into this category. It is as well to take into account that during this period theatres were quite often closed either due to outbreaks of the plague or to the prevailing political and moral climate. Printers, anxious to provide materials that would sell, were not above changing a name or two to enhance sales.

Although Fletcher collaborated most often with Beaumont and Massinger, it is believed that Massinger revised many of the plays some time after their original production. Other collaborators including Nathan Field, William Shakespeare, William Rowley and others also can be seen distinctly in Fletchers' works. Many modern scholars point out that Fletcher had many particular mannerisms but other playwrights would also duplicate these at times so allocating exact contributions of anyone to a play is somewhat of a detective case in many instances. However from the original folio printings or licensing via the Master of the Revels (the statutory licensing authority to approve and censor plays as well a hand in publication and printing of theatrical materials) as well as contemporary notes a fairly precise bibliography of the works can be given with only a few plays lacking substantial authority and provenance.

John Fletcher – A Concise Bibliography

This bibliography gives the most likely date of writing together with when published, revised or licensed by the Master or the Revels (This position within the royal household was originally for royal festivities, ie revels, and later to oversee stage censorship, until this function was transferred to the Lord Chamberlain in 1624).

Solo Plays
The Faithful Shepherdess, pastoral (written 1608–9; printed 1609)
The Tragedy of Valentinian, tragedy (1610–14; 1647)
Monsieur Thomas, comedy (c. 1610–16; 1639)
The Woman's Prize, or The Tamer Tamed, comedy (c. 1611; 1647)
Bonduca, tragedy (1611–14; 1647)
The Chances, comedy (c. 1613–25; 1647)
Wit Without Money, comedy (c. 1614; 1639)
The Mad Lover, tragicomedy (acted 5 January 1617; 1647)
The Loyal Subject, tragicomedy (licensed 16 November 1618; revised 1633; 1647)
The Humorous Lieutenant, tragicomedy (c. 1619; 1647)
Women Pleased, tragicomedy (c. 1619–23; 1647)
The Island Princess, tragicomedy (c. 1620; 1647)
The Wild Goose Chase, comedy (c. 1621; 1652)
The Pilgrim, comedy (c. 1621; 1647)
A Wife for a Month, tragicomedy (licensed 27 May 1624; 1647)
Rule a Wife and Have a Wife, comedy (licensed 19 October 1624; 1640)

Collaborations

With Francis Beaumont
The Woman Hater, comedy (1606; 1607)
Cupid's Revenge, tragedy (c. 1607–12; 1615)
Philaster, or Love Lies a-Bleeding, tragicomedy (c. 1609; 1620)
The Maid's Tragedy, Tragedy (c. 1609; 1619)
A King and No King, tragicomedy (1611; 1619)
The Captain, comedy (c. 1609–12; 1647)
The Scornful Lady, comedy (c. 1613; 1616)
Love's Pilgrimage, tragicomedy (c. 1615–16; 1647)
The Noble Gentleman, comedy (c. 1613; licensed 3 February 1626; 1647)

With Francis Beaumont & Philip Massinger
Thierry & Theodoret, tragedy (c. 1607; 1621)
The Coxcomb, comedy (c. 1608–10; 1647)
Beggars' Bush, comedy (c. 1612–13; revised 1622; 1647)
Love's Cure, comedy (c. 1612–13; revised 1625; 1647)

With Philip Massinger
Sir John van Olden Barnavelt, tragedy (August 1619; MS)
The Little French Lawyer, comedy (c. 1619–23; 1647)
A Very Woman, tragicomedy (c. 1619–22; licensed 6 June 1634; 1655)
The Custom of the Country, comedy (c. 1619–23; 1647)
The Double Marriage, tragedy (c. 1619–23; 1647)
The False One, history (c. 1619–23; 1647)
The Prophetess, tragicomedy (licensed 14 May 1622; 1647)
The Sea Voyage, comedy (licensed 22 June 1622; 1647)
The Spanish Curate, comedy (licensed 24 October 1622; 1647)
The Lovers' Progress or The Wandering Lovers, tragicomedy (licensed 6 December 1623; rev 1634; 1647)
The Elder Brother, comedy (c. 1625; 1637)

With Philip Massinger & Nathan Field
The Honest Man's Fortune, tragicomedy (1613; 1647)
The Queen of Corinth, tragicomedy (c. 1616–18; 1647)
The Knight of Malta, tragicomedy (c. 1619; 1647)

With William Shakespeare
Henry VIII, history (c. 1613; 1623)
The Two Noble Kinsmen, tragicomedy (c. 1613; 1634)
Cardenio, tragicomedy (c. 1613)

With Thomas Middleton & William Rowley
Wit at Several Weapons, comedy (c. 1610–20; 1647)

With William Rowley
The Maid in the Mill (licensed 29 August 1623; 1647).

With Nathan Field
Four Plays, or Moral Representations, in One, morality (c. 1608–13; 1647)

With Philip Massinger, Ben Jonson and George Chapman
Rollo Duke of Normandy, or The Bloody Brother, tragedy (c. 1617; revised 1627–30; 1639)

With James Shirley
The Night Walker, or The Little Thief, comedy (c. 1611; 1640)
The Coronation c. 1635

Uncertain
The Nice Valour, or The Passionate Madman, comedy (c. 1615–25; 1647)
The Laws of Candy, tragicomedy (c. 1619–23; 1647)

The Fair Maid of the Inn, comedy (licensed 22 January 1626; 1647)
The Faithful Friends, tragicomedy (registered 29 June 1660; MS.)

The Nice Valour is possibly by Fletcher revised by Thomas Middleton;

The Fair Maid of the Inn is perhaps a play by Massinger, John Ford, and John Webster, either with or without Fletcher's involvement.

The Laws of Candy has been variously attributed to Fletcher and to John Ford.

The Night-Walker was a Fletcher original, with additions by Shirley for a 1639 production.

Even now there is not absolute certainty on several of the plays. The first Beaumont & Fletcher folio of 1647 contained 35 plays and the second folio of 1679 added a further 18. In total 53 plays.

The first folio included The Masque of the Inner Temple and Gray's Inn (1613), and the second The Knight of the Burning Pestle (1607), widely considered Beaumont's solo works, although the latter was in early editions attributed to both writers. Fletcher himself said that Beaumont was attributed so-authorship of many works that belonged solely to Fletcher or to other collaborators.

One play in the canon, Sir John Van Olden Barnavelt, existed in manuscript and was not published till 1883.

www.ingramcontent.com/pod-product-compliance
Lightning Source LLC
Chambersburg PA
CBHW060120050426
42448CB00010B/1962